REINHOLD PLASTICS
APPLICATIONS SERIES

ACETAL RESINS

RUSSELL B. AKIN

Associate Director
Technical Services Laboratory
E. I. duPont de Nemours & Co., Inc.
Wilmington, Delaware

REINHOLD PUBLISHING CORPORATION

NEW YORK

CHAPMAN & HALL, LTD., LONDON

Printed in the United States of America

Reinhold Plastics Applications Series

The optimum application of plastics continues to be the central theme of this series, even though the scope and character of the series are expanding. Many factors are involved in determining the best plastic for a given end use. One such factor is the method of processing, and for this reason processing books have been introduced.

Since the introduction of this series, a further modification in the original plan has been introduced. Some manuscripts, even though adhering to the precept of brevity, are too long for the established Pilot format; yet they may be of a character which makes inclusion in the series desirable. Such has been the case. With the publication of this volume, which is the twenty-fifth, the series will include both the Pilot and larger formats.

The books, however, will continue to be semi-technical—that is, one need not be a research chemist to understand the various texts. The authors have kept in mind, as probable readers, such industrial men and women as design engineers, equipment manufacturers, producers of packages and packaging machinery, students at technical schools and, of course, all people in the plastics industry—material manufacturers, molders, extruders, fabricators. In addition, it is hoped that each title will appeal to readers in specialized categories. Plastics from which fibers are made may be of interest to tire and fabric manufacturers, and materials favorable for production of sheet may interest handbag and luggage designers. Similarly, some titles may appeal to technical people concerned with paints, magnetic tapes, automobiles, furniture, and even buildings.

With production curves in the plastics field continuing to rise, it is with renewed confidence that this further modification of the series is presented.

HERBERT R. SIMONDS
Editor

TITLES PUBLISHED

FOREWORD

It seems appropriate, in introducing a book on acetal resins, to consider the progress that has been made in structural materials. We have seen, in the decade of the 1950's, the development of the acetal resins and several other greatly improved plastics that combine the easy processing of thermoplastics with the mechanical reliability demanded in durable goods. These are already making an impact on structural design practices.

The evolution of our civilization has been given new direction in the past by the introduction of new materials. Historians have been able easily to catalog the early eras as the "stone age," "bronze age," or "iron age." Future historians will be hard-pressed to view our present "steel-chemical-lightmetal-atomic-plastics age" as anything but the "materials age." What part will structural thermoplastics play in this "materials age"?

The first applications of plastics were novelties. Some uses, particularly in electrical insulation, were unique and could only succeed with the new synthetics. Other ventures were fads or decorative pieces where newness itself was an attraction. After the first wave of success, experiments in substitution began. Despite the usual quota of growing pains, plastics gained in that phase a firm hold in several fields. One natural and successful conquest was substitution for plastic-like materials, such as natural fibers, elastomers, films and surface coatings. Another qualified but important success was in low-cost expendable items, the much abused toy, sports equipment and houseware markets. In totally unique applications, electrical insulation and plastic foams, plastics earned another secure outlet.

The materials shortages of World War II hastened the use of plastics, as substitute materials, in more rugged structural applications. The first military applications, conservative but expensive, showed promise in housing, aircraft structures and other mechanical functions. However, enthusiasm and optimism soon led to a series of disappointing experiments in designing with plastics. It became apparent that only a limited number of thermoset plastics could be used safely in conventional structural designs. Most thermoplastics were entirely unsuitable. With advances in processing, it also became evident that thermoplastics could often give the most favorable costs.

The introduction in the 1950's of rubber-reinforced plastics, nylon, rigid vinyls, tailor-made polyolefins, polycarbonates and acetal resins offered a variety of thermoplastic materials that have desirable application properties. Being thermoplastic, they come closest to the designer's ideal of providing any required shape in an economical and fast manufacturing process—injection molding, thermoforming or blow molding. They also exhibit the major advantages of plastics—broad raw material base and moderate cost, appearance, warmth, resilience, lightweight, and so on—while possessing reasonable strength. The price that must be paid for this bonanza is high. To take full advantage of those good features, we must grow in education and knowledge. We need to discard our preconceived and traditional concepts of design and improve our precision in estimating design requirements. We need to develop new ways to evaluate materials. Finally, we must recognize how different are plastics from steel and aluminum and ceramics and other familiar materials.

Thermoplastic materials, even more than thermosets, are subject to the limitations of the loosely combined organic

polymers from which they are made. Mechanical properties
are profoundly affected by changes of temperature or by
exposure to chemical environments and prolonged mechanical
loadings. Properties are changed drastically by differences
in processing conditions. Rate of loading has an important
influence on strength. Unexpected failures of structural
plastics have most often been caused by inadequate knowledge of those factors. All thermoplastic materials have
temperature limitations, both high and low, that are no more
than several hundred degrees Fahrenheit from room temperature. All thermoplastics tend to creep and deform or suffer
fatigue damage and fracture on long-term applications of
high mechanical loads. Specific chemical environments, not
all of them unusual, can interact with load or temperature
effects and reduce the useful design range even further.
Those limitations pose serious questions since long life, by
definition, is important in durable goods and structures.
The designer needs to know the conditions of his application with greater certainty than ever before. He also must
learn how to interpret new kinds of property data that do
not fit into the classical design equations.

In this book, Dr. Russell Akin reviews those problems
and some of the new design concepts, using acetal resins as
an example. His discussion points out the obstacles with
honesty but indicates that there are answers to some of the
problems.

Substantial progress has already been made in the structural use of thermoplastics. Major household appliances,
automobiles and the construction industry all furnish successful examples. Growing quantities of thermoplastics are
being used, with advantage, in bearings, handles, equipment
housings and in corrosion-resistant ware. Designers are gain-
ing first an intuitive and then an informed knowledge of
the necessary new design concepts.

Field experience is accumulating and confidence is growing with various devices under a wide variety of use conditions. Material suppliers are beginning to recognize the need and their responsibility to furnish comprehensive property data. New approaches to testing of thermoplastic materials now under study are starting to give correlations between basic material properties and end-use results. We are learning to choose the best combinations of properties of versatile, tailor-made materials for use in the structures, equipment and devices that will make our lives easier in the future.

We need to view this field with a mature sense of proportion. We can no more expect to see an "all-plastic" house or automobile or appliance in the future than we expect today to have an "all-wood" or an "all-steel" house. The structures of the future will, as always, be "all-materials" systems. Each material, traditional or new, will furnish its best features to the combination. You can be certain that the synthetic structural thermoplastics, such as acetal resins, will play an important role.

JOHN V. SCHMITZ

Major Appliance Chemistry Laboratory,
General Electric Company,
Appliance Park, Louisville, Ky.

February, 1962

CONTENTS

1. CHEMICAL HISTORY AND SYNTHESIS

This book discusses properties, design features and uses of a new plastic of increasing industrial importance—acetal resins. The term *acetal* refers to an oxygen atom which joins the repeating units of the structure in an ether rather than ester type of link. There is a wide variety of units and more than one type may be used in a single plastic. The acetal resins discussed here became commercially available early in 1960, and engineering data are limited to the plastic made as a linear polymer of oxymethylene. However, to indicate modifications which may be developed, some literature and patent references are cited on other compositions.

Among users of structural parts, acetal resin is a new name and the currently accepted definition is a stiff, tough material processable by standard injection and extrusion techniques. Hence, to avoid misinterpretation, the following acetal resins are *not* included in the usage of "acetal resin" in this book:

Polyvinyl butyral, used in laminating automotive safety glass:

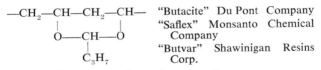

$$-CH_2-CH-CH_2-CH-$$
$$\hspace{1.2cm} | \hspace{1.5cm} |$$
$$\hspace{0.6cm} O——CH——O$$
$$\hspace{2cm} |$$
$$\hspace{2cm} C_3H_7$$

"Butacite" Du Pont Company
"Saflex" Monsanto Chemical Company
"Butvar" Shawinigan Resins Corp.

Polyvinyl formal, used as wire enamel:

$$-CH_2-CH-CH_2-CH-$$
$$\hspace{1.2cm} | \hspace{1.5cm} |$$
$$\hspace{0.6cm} O——CH_2——O$$

"Formvar" Shawinigan Resins Corp.

1

This volume deals primarily with the acetal resins which are high molecular weight, stable, linear polymers of formaldehyde, CH_2O. The structure of the acetal resin is:

$$H-O-(CH_2-O-CH_2-O)_x H$$

where terminal groups are derived from controlled amounts of water (H—O—H), and the x denotes a large (typically 1500) number of formaldehyde units linked in head-to-tail fashion. To increase thermal and chemical resistance, terminal groups may be converted to esters or ethers. This structure differs from other polymers of formaldehyde such as trioxane because the molecules are long and linear (unbranched and of relatively narrow cross-section). They pack closely and provide a high degree of stiffness, toughness and chemical resistance.

Other oxymethylenes may be used, in which one or both hydrogens of formaldehyde may be replaced by organic radicals such as methyl or benzyl. Polymers from such starting materials have not yet been offered commercially.

At the time of this writing, there is a single commercial member of this acetal family, "Delrin," made by E. I. du Pont de Nemours & Company, Inc. One other similar acetal resin, "Celcon," of Celanese Corporation, has been announced as a copolymer of formaldehyde with an unidentified comonomer.

When choosing a material, the design engineer likes to know what other uses have been tried. The Appendix tabulates some applications which became established during the first two years of commercial sale of acetal molding powder; many of them had been studied for several years previously with experimental resin. As a guide to effect of environment or economy, the material displaced by acetal is named in many cases. Emphatically, this does not mean that the material change was made without redesign, nor that performance and cost were both improved.

Polymerization of formaldehyde has been known for a century, but until recently all polymers were brittle and largely reverted to gaseous formaldehyde when they were heated in attempts to mold. Polymers that were tough (yielding films capable of repeated creasing after a week at 105°C) and thermally stable (less than one per cent weight loss per minute at 222°C) were first described and patented by MacDonald (U.S. Patent 2,768,994, to Du Pont). Polymers may be prepared by passing pure anhydrous formaldehyde into agitated liquid hydrocarbon. Polymerization may be catalyzed by amines, phosphines, metal alkyls, metal carbonyls, or metal halides.

The literature on formaldehyde polymerization, synthesis steps and properties of useful acetal resins is summarized in a series of papers * by authors of the Du Pont Company. An extensive review of journal and patent literature is by Kern, Cherdron and Jaacks.†

Further improvements in thermal and chemical stability can be achieved by converting the hydroxyl groups at end of acetal resin to ester or ether groups, or by incorporating polyamide resins (British Patent 860,410 to Du Pont Company).

The infinite variety of copolymers possible is indicated in British Patent 807,589 to Du Pont Company, which describes block copolymers of formaldehyde with monomers or prepolymers of other materials capable of providing active hydrogens, such as alkylene glycols, polythiols, vinyl acetate-acrylic acid copolymers, or reduced butadiene/acrylonitrile polymers.

Celanese Corporation has claimed linear acetal polymers

---

* *Journal of Applied Polymer Science,* **1,** 158-191 (1959).

† *Angewandte Chemie,* **73,** 177-186 (1961).

TABLE 1.1. TYPICAL PROPERTIES OF STRUCTURAL THERMOPLASTICS, BY ASTM TESTS AT 73°F AND 50 PER CENT RELATIVE HUMIDITY.

	Acetal	Nylon 66	Nylon 6	Carbonate	ABS High Impact	ABS Medium Impact
Tensile strength, psi	10,000	11,200	9,700	9,500	5,100	8,800
Elongation, %	15	300	260	90	100	20
Flex modulus, psi	410,000	175,000	140,000	375,000	240,000	450,000
Izod impact, ft-lb per inch notch	1.4	2.0	5.0	12	6	1.5
Heat deformation temp. at 66 psi, °F	338	433	370	293	208	215
Specific gravity	1.42	1.14	1.13	1.2	1.02	1.07
Rockwell hardness, R	120	108	93	118	87	118
Water absorption, % 24 hour	0.25	1.5	1.8	0.3	0.2	0.3

Acetal: formaldehyde homopolymer.
Nylon 66: hexamethylene adipamide.
Nylon 6: caprolactam.
Carbonate: from bisphenol-A.
ABS: acrylonitrile-butadiene-styrene copolymer.

from trioxane by catalysis with alkane sulfonic acids (U.S. Patent 2,947,727) and metal chlorides (U.S. Patent 2,947,728).

Several families of thermoplastics are now serving well in structural uses. Table 1.1 provides comparison of some physical properties in order to orient the reader. Each of these types is available in a range of compositions, and other properties must be considered. For instance, repeated impact may give very different relative rating from a single impact value, and minor changes in chemical environment may greatly change a given physical property. For nearly all mechanical uses, prototypes should be machined before molding in quantity is undertaken.

2. PROPERTIES

This chapter is divided into four major sections, as follows:

    A. Physical properties, as usually determined by procedures of the American Society for Testing Materials.

    B. Chemical properties, including permeability and toxicology.

    C. Electrical properties, by ASTM methods.

    D. Design data for engineering calculation.

Section D discusses properties and concepts for design of structural parts. These procedures have not been described elsewhere; they employ the usual formulas for stress analysis of metal parts, modified only to account for the time-dependency of properties of plastics. Additional design data are given in Chapters 4 and 5.

As with most plastics, it is a combination of properties—rather than a single property—which results in commercial utility. In the case of acetals the salient properties are high stiffness; retention of stiffness at elevated temperature and in the presence of organic liquids or moisture; high tensile and impact strength; good bearing properties and resistance to fatigue; high softening temperature; and adaptability to injection molding due to high fluidity when molten and rapid setting upon cooling. The majority of applications are those requiring resistance to, or recovery from, deformation. Examples are piping and hose fittings, combs, fasteners, and many types of bearings and gears which go through repeated cyclic loadings.

A. PHYSICAL PROPERTIES

Data on major physical properties, by standard ASTM tests are in Table 2.1.

Elongation and Tensile Strength

At room temperature, elongation is 15 per cent and tensile strength is 10,000 psi with no true yield point. At higher temperatures, particularly around 212°F, there is a well-defined yield point and elongation ranges from 350 to 500 per cent. Stress is plotted versus strain for three temperatures in Figure 2.1.

Impact Strength

As shown in Table 2.1, Izod impact strength does not fall off abruptly at sub-zero temperatures, as it does with plastics which achieve room-temperature toughness by incorporation of plasticizer. The values given here are for bars notched by machining. Molded notches have smoother surface, and at 73°F show 1.7 foot-pounds per inch. When a bar with a molded notch is filled by gating at both ends, the notch is at the weld line, and the value is 1.6 foot-pounds, indicative of good welding because of high fluidity of the molten plastic. Unnotched Izod strength is 20.5 foot-pounds per inch. This difference between unnotched and notched specimens emphasizes the need to eliminate sharp corners and rough surfaces to achieve maximum resistance to impact.

For design purposes, the impact strength of acetal is not significantly affected by temperature (Figure 2.2) or humidity (Figure 2.3).

Standard impact data indicate usefulness of acetal for such

TABLE 2.1. PHYSICAL PROPERTIES OF ACETAL RESIN.

Property	Units	ASTM. No.	Av. Values For "Delrin" *	
			500	150
Elogation, −68°F	%	D638	13	38
73°F	%	D638	15	75
158°F	%	D638	330	460
Impact strength, Izod, −40°F	ft lb/in.	D256	1.2	1.8
73°F	ft lb/in.	D256	1.4	2.3
Tensile strength and yield point, −68°F	psi	D638	14,700	
73°F	psi	D638	10,000	
158°F	psi	D638	7,500	
Compressive stress at 1% deformation	psi	D695	5,200	
Compressive stress at 10% deformation	psi		18,000	
Flexural modulus, 73°F	psi	D790	410,000	
170°F	psi	D790	190,000	
250°F	psi	D790	90,000	
100% relative humidity, 73°F	psi	D790	360,000	
Flexural strength	psi	D790	14,100	
Shear strength	psi	D732	9,510	
Heat deflection temperature, 264 psi	°F	D648	212	
66 psi	°F	D648	338	
Fatigue endurance limit,				
70°F, 50 to 100% relative humidity	psi		5,000	
150°F, 100% relative humidity	psi		3,000	
Water absorption, 24 hours immersion	%	D570	0.4	
equilibrium, 50% relative humidity	%	D570	0.2	
equilibrium, immersion, 77°F	%		0.9	

Property	ASTM	Units	Value
Specific gravity	D792		1.425
Rockwell hardness	D785		M94, R120
Flammability	D635	in./min.	1.1
Melting point (crystalline)		°F	347
Flow temperature	D569	°F	363
Deformation under load (2000 psi at 122°F)	D621	%	0.5
Coefficient of linear thermal expansion	D696	per °F	4.5×10^{-5}
Taber abrasion (1000 gm load, CS-17 wheel)	D1044	mg/1000 cycles	20
Thermal conductivity		Btu/hr/sq ft/°F/in.	1.6
Specific heat		Btu/lb/°F	0.35
Modulus of rigidity		psi	178,000
Poisson's ratio			0.38
Dielectric constant, 73°F, 10^2-10^5 cps	D150		3.7
Dissipation factor, 73°F, 10^2-10^5 cps	D150		.004
Dielectric strength, short time	D149	V/mil	500
Volume resistivity, dry	D257	ohm-cm	6×10^{14}
saturated	D257	ohm-cm	2×10^{13}
Arc resistance	D495	sec.	129 (burns)**

Permeability			P Factor at 73°F
Water		gm loss/24 hr/100 in.² area/mil thickness. Determined on bottles with 35-50 mil wall thickness.	1.9
Ethanol			0.2
"Freon" 12-114 (20/80)			0.2
Methyl salicylate			0.3

* These values are representative of those obtained under standard ASTM conditions and should not be used to design parts which function under different conditions. Since they are average values they should not be used as minimums for material specifications.

** Does not track.

Acetal Resins

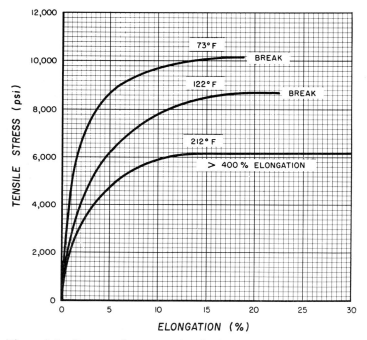

Figure 2.1. Stress-strain curve—(tension). Based on original cross section using a strain rate of 0.2 in./min. ASTM No. D-638.

things as auto door-latch wedges, freezer latch rollers and clothespins, where ability to withstand sudden stress is important. A different kind of toughness is that shown by resistance to bending around small radius. Such a test shows significant difference between acetal and a 66 nylon which has similar stiffness. A bar of acetal ⅛-inch thick can be bent 90° around a ⅛-inch mandrel, while a bar of dry 66 nylon can be bent 180°. Acetal can be bent 180° around a ⅜-inch mandrel. Acetal is indicated where toughness is needed for strength and rigidity; nylon is preferred where toughness in the sense of resilience from impact is required.

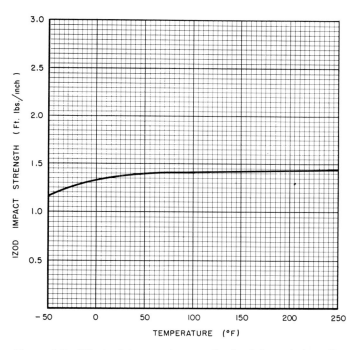

Figure 2.2. Effect of temperature on the Izod impact strength.

Hardness and Resistance to Abrasion

Hardness tests are usually a measure of the amount of indentation under specific unit loadings. For acetal, Rockwell hardness is M94 or R120, and is only slightly reduced by moisture absorption or temperature over the normal operating range.

The abrasion resistance of plastics is not so well indicated by indentation procedures as it is for metals. Where resistance to abrasion is required, tests closely simulating the proposed use should be run. Table 2.2 shows weight loss of

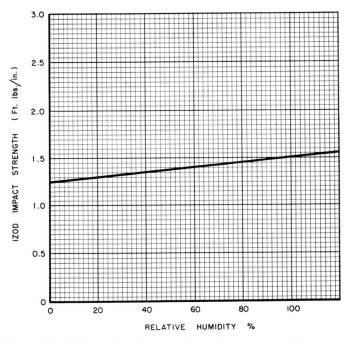

Figure 2.3. Effect of moisture on Izod impact strength at room
temperature.

various plastics by different types of abrasion tests; the loss
given is relative to weight lost by 66 nylon in the same test.
It should be noted that the kind of test makes considerable
difference in the results.

The data of Table 2.2 were obtained as follows:

(1) Taber abrasion tests were made with a CS-17 wheel
and a 1,000-gram load. The plastic test pieces were conditioned at 23°C and 50 per cent relative humidity.

(2) Ball mill abrasion tests were made by rolling 2 x ½ x ⅛-
inch bars in a 5-inch Abbé ball mill with 25 "Borundum"

TABLE 2.2. COMPARATIVE WEIGHT LOSS OF VARIOUS MATERIALS IN DIFFERENT ABRASION TESTS.

	Taber	Ball Mill	Wire Drag	Sander
Nylon 66	1	1	1	1
"Delrin"	2–5	4–6	5–6	3–4
Polystyrene (several types)	9–26	15–20	35	—
Terpolymer of styrene, butadiene, and acrylonitrile	9	10–20	—	—
Cellulose acetate	9–10	—	—	—
Cellulose acetate butyrate	9–15	10–20	15	—
Polymethyl methacrylate	2–5	10–20	20	—
Polyvinylidene chloride	9–12	—	—	—
Melamine formaldehyde (molded)	—	15–20	—	—
Phenol formaldehyde (moldings)	4–12	—	—	—
Hard rubber	—	10	—	4
Die cast aluminum	—	11	—	4–5
Mild steel	—	15–20	—	—

Each number represents the ratio of weight lost to 66 nylon in the same time.

balls and 500 ml water. In various instances, molded objects were substituted for test bars, the "Borundum" balls were replaced by steel balls, and the water was omitted without substantial change in the relative results.

(3) Wire drag abrasion tests were conducted by pulling a continuous loop of fine resistance wire (spirally wrapped on a cord) over a cylindrical test piece. The cord was held at a constant tension and pulled over the test piece at about 70 feet per minute. The depth of the groove was measured after 30 minutes.

(4) In the sander abrasion test, football cleats of various materials were pushed with a constant force against the belt of a wet sander.

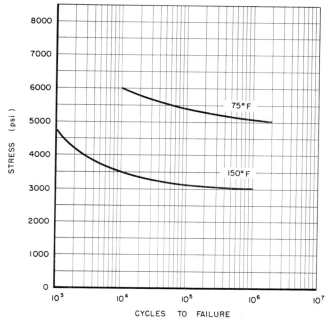

Figure 2.4. Fatigue data for "Delrin" at 100 per cent R. H. Stress completely reversed tensile and compressive at 1800 cycles per minute.

Fatigue

When parts are to be loaded statically, the yield strength (chosen between points A and B, depending on duration (Figure 2.9a) is the usual basis for estimating performance. However, all known materials ultimately fail on repeated application of stresses lower than their static yield strength. This phenomenon is called fatigue failure, and demands a design basis other than yield strength for gears or other parts subjected to repeated loading.

Experimentally, it was found that there is a stress value below which acetal will not fail, however many times the load is applied. The behavior is like that of ferrous alloys, and similarly the value is called the fatigue endurance limit. Designing below the fatigue endurance limit is the best assurance that the part will perform satisfactorily even though the load is applied millions of times, as on tooth of a gear.

Typical data were obtained on a Sonntag-Universal Machine, which flexes a beam in tension and compression. Figure 2.4 shows maximum stresses to failure. Thus far, effects of frequency appear negligible in the range from 56 to 1800 cycles per second. No adverse effect would be expected at lower frequencies. Higher frequencies might be expected to change properties due to generation of heat. Moisture content has not been found to be a significant factor.

As with impact testing, the geometry of the piece and the presence of notches exert tremendous effect on fatigue limit. Figure 2.4 was obtained on a completely reversed cycle, full tension to full compression. Where only one of these loadings is cycled, fatigue limits 30 per cent higher are usually achieved.

B. CHEMICAL PROPERTIES

Among thermoplastics, only fluorocarbon polymers show greater resistance toward organic solvents than homopolymer acetal. Below 160°F, no effective organic solvent for acetal has been found. Over 400 solvents, representing 27 classes of compounds, were tried without finding any which gave as much as a 1 per cent solution. At higher temperatures some solution occurs. Phenolic types have greatest solvent power. Over several months, dry, warm chlorophenol or benzyl alcohol solutions showed no reduction in molecular weight as indicated by solution viscosity; when containing water, chlorophenol showed some lowering of viscosity, apparently due to hydrolysis.

Table 2.3 shows the effects of various organic solvents, Table 2.4 those of some inorganic chemicals. Acetal should not be used in strong acids, strong alkalies, or oxidants.

Acetal Resins

TABLE 2.3. RESISTANCE TO ORGANIC CHEMICALS.

	Tensile Strength		Weight		Length	
			% Change in 12 Months			
Reagent	Room Temp.	158°F	Room Temp.	158°F	Room Temp.	158°F
50% Igepal	+2	−58	−1.8	+0.1	+0.05	−1.21
"Nujol"	+1	+2	+0.3	−0.5	−0.08	−0.37
"Uniflo" motor oil 10W30	—	+3	—	−0.2	—	−0.30
Carbon tetrachloride	−3	−7*	+1.2	+5.7*	+0.30	−0.25*
100% Ethyl alcohol	−5	−5*	+2.2	+1.9*	+0.81	+1.00*
Acetone	−5	−7*	+4.9	+2.6*	+0.91	+1.08*
5% Acetic acid	0	−8*	+0.8	−2.6*	+0.15	−0.22*
Toluene	−7	−7*	+2.6	+2.8*	+1.20	+1.20*
"Lockheed" 21 brake fluid	—	−23	—	+0.9	—	+0.29
Ethyl acetate	−7	−7*	+2.7	+2.9*	+1.35	+1.10*

Test Conditions:

1. Bars were completely immersed in solvent for time indicated.
2. Tests were made by standard ASTM procedures at room temperature immediately after removal of bars from solvents.

* Because of difficulties in carrying out the test these samples were tested at 122°F instead of the higher temperature.

TABLE 2.4. RESISTANCE TO INORGANIC CHEMICALS.

	Tensile Strength		Weight		Length	
Reagent	Room Temp.	158°F	Room Temp.	158°F	Room Temp.	158°F
30% Sulfuric acid	—>30	—	—48	—	—	—
10% Nitric acid	—>30	—	—70	—	−1.00	—
10% Hydrochloric acid	—>30	—	—84	—	−.191	—
10% Sodium hydroxide	0.0	—	+0.01	1	+0.02	—
10% Sodium chloride	0.0	+1.0	+0.05	+0.02	+0.01	0.00
Buffer soln., pH 4	—	—>60	—	—>20	—	—
Buffer soln., pH 7	—	−1.0	—	−0.05	—	−0.22
Buffer soln., pH 10	—	−3.2	—	−0.83	—	+0.02

% Change in 6 months

Test Conditions:

1. Bars were completely immersed in solvent for time indicated.
2. Tests were made by standard ASTM procedures at room temperature immediately after removal from solvents.

Below pH 4 or above pH 9 hydrolytic attack will first etch the surface, then reduce molecular weight and cause embrittlement. Under milder conditions, tests should be used to determine suitability.

Stress-cracking of acetal has not been encountered in organic solvents, although strong acids will craze areas under stress from either bending or molding strain. Bars of acetal stressed to just below the breaking point have not shown crazing in toluene, carbon tetrachloride, acetone, new or used motor oils, brake fluid, buffered solutions of pH 4 and pH 10, 5 per cent acetic acid, 20 per cent phenol, 37 per cent formaldehyde, 10 per cent sodium chloride or 25 per cent "Igepal" detergent (which actively cracks stressed polyethylene). The only adverse effect was staining of the stressed area by used motor oil.

Stain resistance is good. During a week at room temperature acetal was not stained by tea, coffee, catsup, lipstick or oleomargarine. Hot coffee will stain acetal, but markedly less than it stains 66 nylon.

Contact with foods appears to present neither toxicity nor taste problems. Feeding tests of rats where "Delrin" acetal resin comprised 25 per cent of diet for ninety days showed no significant difference in body weight or clinical history. Prolonged animal feeding tests are under way. Until these are completed and approval is obtained from the Food and Drug Administration, acetal is not proposed for packaging food. Dishware, coffee cups and other household items perform very well, with good resistance to abrasion and dishwashers. The amount of formaldehyde released in such use is less than with quality melamine dishware. Acetal has been found not to irritate or sensitize intact skin, and to be only mildly irritating to abraded skin of guinea pigs.

Extraction tests have been run by Du Pont on pipe and film made from "Delrin" acetal resin. In water at 212°F,

¾-inch pipe would provide 1.04 parts per million of formaldehyde; at 60°F, the estimated formaldehyde concentration would be less than .003 part per million. As tomatoes have 16 parts per million and spinach from 10 to 25, acetal presents no toxic hazard. The National Sanitation Foundation has also tested "Delrin," and granted its seal of approval. Used daily for four years in homes, dishware of acetal has presented no problem; it does scratch more readily than melamine dishware under a sharp knife.

Permeability is less than that of polyethylene toward hydrocarbons, esters, and halogenated hydrocarbons used as aerosol propellants. Permeability toward water vapor is significantly higher than for polyethylene. Permeability data are in Table 2.5.

TABLE 2.5. PERMEABILITY BY ORGANIC LIQUIDS.

Liquid	"Delrin" Loss/yr (grams)	P Factor *	Low-density Polyethylene P Factor *	High-density Polyethylene P Factor *
Methyl salicylate	0.51	0.27	9.1	2.0
Toluene	1.28	0.65	566.0	150.0
Turpentine	0.04	0.023	47.0	3.0
Methanol	—	—	3.6	0.4
Ethanol	0.40	0.22	—	—
Water	7.7	3.5	0.35	—
"Perclene" (chlorinated hydrocarbon)	0.40	0.23	—	—
"Freon" 12/114	0.6	0.33	—	—

Test Conditions:

Containers: Sealed 4 oz. Boston round bottles, blow molded, 35 mils thick.
Temperature: 73°F.
Humidity: 50% relative humidity.

* P factor is defined as the grams lost per 24 hours per 100 square inch area per mil wall thickness. This factor allows the calculation of the loss that can be expected from any given bottle.

As may be seen from the preceding chemical resistance data, strong aqueous acid or alkali will degrade acetal resins. With water alone, hydrolysis is not usually a factor to consider in strength or dimensional stability, and plumbing fixtures show excellent performance. Parts have been autoclaved for one hundred 15-minute cycles in 250°F steam without significant loss in strength, toughness or dimensional stability.

On going from bone dry or as-molded state to equilibrium moisture content (0.2 per cent moisture at 73°F at 50 per cent relative humidity) acetal expands 0.1 per cent, or one mil per inch of length. At 73°F complete immersion shows 0.8 per cent absorption by weight, and dimensional increase is 0.4 per cent, or 4 mils per inch. Extensive data for designers are presented in Figures 2.4-2.8.

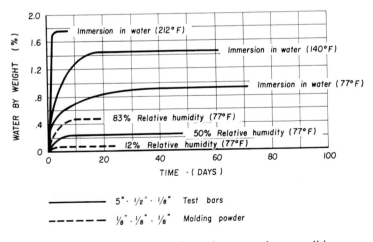

Figure 2.5. Rate of water absorption at various conditions.

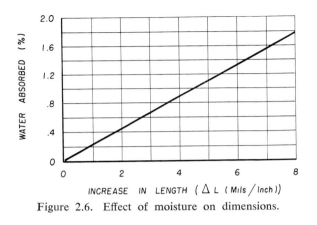

Figure 2.6. Effect of moisture on dimensions.

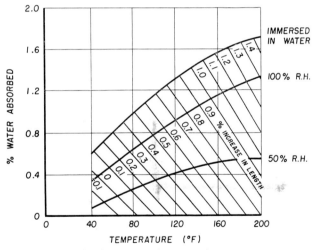

Figure 2.7. Effect of moisture and temperature on dimensions.

Note : To find the change in dimensions resulting from environmental changes subtract the "per cent increase in length" figure found at the second temperature—humidity condition:—e.g. to go from 77°F and 0% water (the as-molded condition which was chosen as the reference point) to 100°F and 100%, a dimensional change of 0.45% will be observed.

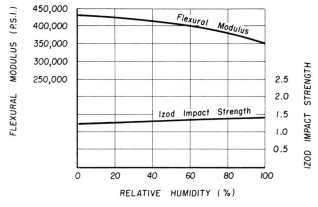

Figure 2.8. Effect of moisture on flexural modulus and impact strength at 80°F.

Acetal, like all thermoplastics except fluorocarbons, is affected by ultraviolet radiation. Prolonged exposure may induce chalking of the surface, and will reduce molecular weight with gradual embrittlement. Best exposure resistance comes from incorporation of well-dispersed carbon black. Colored compositions maintain properties fairly well, but the surface will chalk on outdoor exposure and present stocks should be considered to have only fair weatherability. Ordinary window glass filters out ultraviolet, so interior service is likely to be good.

Acetal does not lose its properties when buried underground, nor is there record of attack by fungi, rodents, or insects.

There is no significant loss in physical properties when acetal is exposed to air continuously at 180°F, or intermittently at 250°F.

Acetal will burn slowly when ignited by flame. The standard ASTM burning test D635 rates acetal as slow-burning

(1.1 inch per minute), about like acrylics, styrene and polyethylene. The flame is soot-free and of very low luminosity;
small flames are readily extinguished, as the heat of combus-
tion is lower than for most plastics. For behavior in electric
arc, see Section C.

C. ELECTRICAL PROPERTIES

Although the fact is not widely appreciated, most electrical
uses of plastics depend on the mechanical rather than on the
electrical properties of a given material. Thus, comparison
of various polymers for electrical use should include mechanical and thermal behavior. Electrical properties of acetal are
given in Table 2.6.

Dielectric constant and dissipation factor are uniform over
a wide frequency range, and are lower than those of cellulose
esters, nylon, vinyl chloride and impact styrenes. Polycar-

TABLE 2.6. ELECTRICAL PROPERTIES.

	ASTM No.	Value
Dielectric strength,		.125 in. thick 500 V/mil
short time	D-149	.010 1700 V/mil
Volume resistivity	D-257	6×10^{14} ohm/cm (0.2 % water)
		4.6×10^{13} (0.9 % water)
Surface resistivity	D-257	10^{16} ohm
Arc resistance	D-495	129 sec. (burns)*
Dielectric constant,		
73°F	D-150	10^2 cps—3.7
		10^3 cps—3.7
		10^4 cps—3.7
Dissipation factor,		
73°F	D-150	10^2 cps—0.004
		10^3 cps—0.004
		10^4 cps—0.004

* Does not track. Evolved gases do not usually ignite.

bonate, polystyrene and polyethylene have lower values and show less change with frequency.

Maximum continuous use temperature of 185°F (for stiffness and toughness) limits acetal to Class O (194°F, 90°C), service rating, or in some designs to Class A (221°F, 105°C).

Arc resistance tests (ASTM D495-56T) show neither carbonizing nor tracking. Times to develop hole were:

Specimen Thickness (mil)	Time (sec.)
10	125
20	140
30	190

In these tests, the arc decomposed acetal and the evolved gas did not ignite. When arc was cut off, gas evolution ceased.

D. DESIGN DATA FOR ENGINEERING AND STRUCTURAL USE

This section shows how parts made of acetal may be designed with confidence for dimensional stability and support of loads. The procedures are applicable to rigid plastics in general. It is remarkable how little of this information has appeared in the plastics literature, in view of the successful use of acetal in a wide variety of applications. Accordingly, the treatment here is rather extensive as to procedures, although the examples are restricted to acetal.

It is practical to design a structural part in plastics with the same stress formulas as for structural metals and concrete. The only modification is to employ data which allow for the effect of time on deformation caused by load or environment. This time-dependency of deformation is called creep, whether in tension or compression. Satisfactory performance of structural parts will be achieved only when there is applied to selection of material and design of part, an adequate knowledge of the environment and the manner, magnitude and duration of loading. Factors of safety are about the same as for cast metals. They are necessarily based on judgment and cannot be generalized to cover all conditions. A prototype should be machined and tested under actual use, especially when only an estimate can be made of the loadings.

Physical property data essential to design are presented. These are usually determined by ASTM test equipment operated over such range of load, temperature and time as to produce data of value to structural designers.

Illustration of behavior and presentation of design data are best provided by graphing stress (load) versus strain (deformation) of ASTM samples. The following stress-strain curves (Figures 2.1 and 2.9-2.18) are shown here for quick reference in design calculating:

Stress-strain Behavior

Thermoplastic materials submitted to tensile stress at ASTM-recommended rates of strain undergo deformation (strain) according to one of three rather well-defined behaviors shown in Figure 2.9a, b and c. Materials of gradual yield are represented by Figure 2.9a; such are acetal, polyethylene, or moisture-conditioned 66 nylon. Materials of abrupt yield are represented by Figure 2.9b, i.e., dry, as-molded 66 nylon. Methacrylate molding compositions fracture at low strain rates before yielding, and are represented by Figure 2.9c.

The stress-strain curve for acetal differs with temperatures of test (see Figure 2.1). Below 215°F, total elongation is 15 per cent with no sharply defined yield point. At higher temperatures there is a well-defined yield point with considerable elongation. In view of high stiffness and strength of

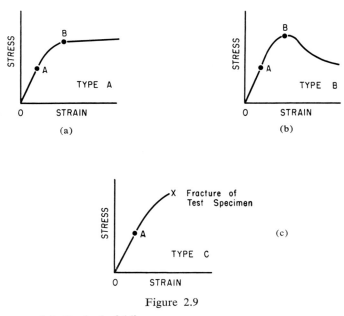

Figure 2.9

(a) Gradual yielding.
(b) Abrupt yielding.
(c) Fracture occurs at low strains before yielding.

acetal, the yield point and ultimate tensile strength (point of breakage) are the same for practical design purposes.

Stress-strain curves in both compression and tension (Figure 2.10) show that for strains larger than 1 per cent the compressive yield point is higher than the tensile yield point. This means that for given deflection, parts loaded in compression will require less material.

Plot of yield point versus temperature (Figure 2.11) show remarkably linear relation from −45 to 230°F. Design calculations should employ the yield point for highest temperature which the part may reach in service.

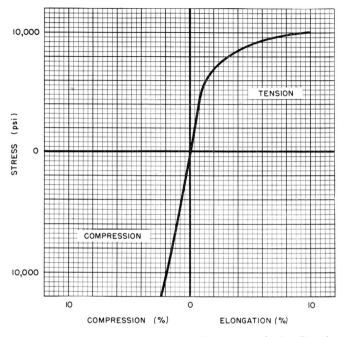

Figure 2.10. Stress-strain curve—(tension-compression). Based on original cross section using a strain rate of 0.2 in./min. at 73°F.

Values of modulus of elasticity versus temperature (Figure 2.12) may be used for either tension or compression, as these values are nearly equal. As moisture affects modulus to only a slight extent, it may be neglected in calculations.

As an example of use of data in Figure 2.12, consider a part under short-term tensile stress of 3,000 psi at 125°F in air at 50 per cent relative humidity. From this figure modulus is read to be 300,000 psi. The unit strain is then 3,000 divided by 300,000, or .01 inch per inch.

Torsion modulus, or modulus in shear, is 178,000 psi at

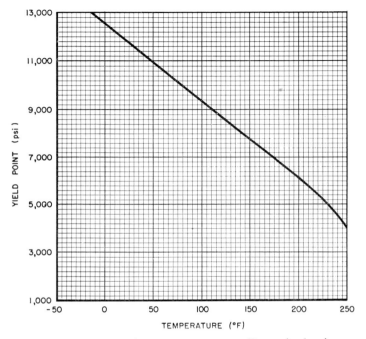

Figure 2.11. Yield point *vs.* temperature. Determined using a strain rate of 0.2 in./min. at various temperatures.

73°F. Variation with temperature and humidity are about the same as for modulus of elasticity.

Creep, Cold Flow, Apparent Modulus Concept

When a material is subjected to continuous load, there is a continued deformation with time which is called creep. This phenomenon occurs with metals at elevated temperatures. With most plastics the deformation can be significant even at room temperature; hence it is frequently called cold flow. Creep is the total deformation under stress after a

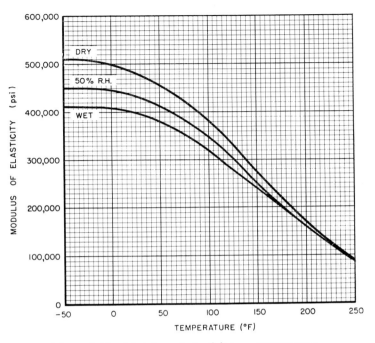

Figure 2.12. Modulus of elasticity *vs.* temperature.

specified time in a given environment. Figure 2.13 shows tensile creep data at 160°F for various loads and times. The curves show initial strain or deformation as soon as load is applied. The modulus of elasticity is determined from this instantaneous deformation. Following this initial strain, the part continues to deform, but at decreasing rate.

The designer should consider two distinct regions of the stress-strain curve. In the first region (line *OA* in Figure 2.9a)—elastic design principles may be applied: strain is instantly apparent upon loading, and recovery is essentially complete and instantaneous upon removal of stress. The

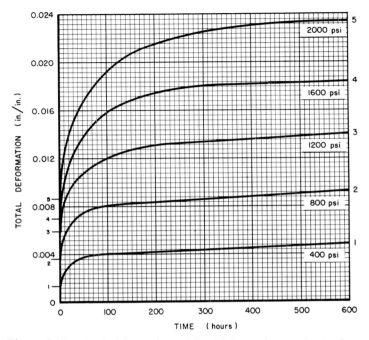

Figure 2.13. Total deformation of "Delrin" *vs.* time under load at 160°F and 80 per cent R.H.

Note: Points indicated on the ordinate show the initial strain for curves 1-5, respectively.

second region (around point *B* in Figure 2.9a) is that of the yield point: it is the design value used when fracture or failure due to large deformation is of prime concern. Depending on rate of loading or duration of load, the yield strength may be selected as the stress at some point between *A* and *B*.

To translate creep data into usable design practice the concept of "apparent modulus" has been employed. The linear portion (*OA*, Figure 2.9a) of the stress-strain curve shows the behavior until Hooke's law is no longer valid. Careful study

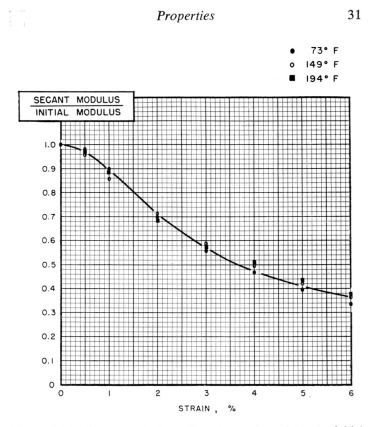

Figure 2.14. Decrease of the ratio of secant modulus to initial modulus with increasing strain.

of data for thermoplastics shows that there is no linear portion of the stress-strain curve, but rather increasing deviation from linearity as strain increases. Published data show elastic modulus E_0 as the slope of a line tangent to the low-strain portion of the curve.

If a point approaching B on Figure 2.9a is selected as the amount of strain tolerable in a part, then the slope of line

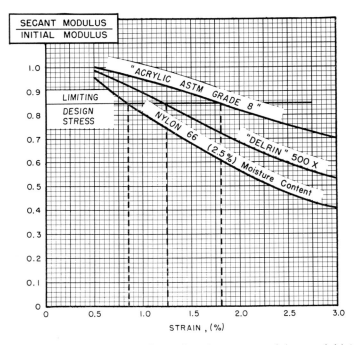

Figure 2.15. Decrease of the ratio of secant modulus to initial modulus with increasing strain (73°F).

OB is the secant modulus, E_s. The secant modulus decreases with increasing strain; that is, this modulus becomes smaller as deformation becomes greater. Figure 2.14 plots ratio E_s/E_0 versus strain; at three temperatures, the ratio for acetal remains practically constant. Figure 2.14 emphasizes that E_0, the initial modulus becomes a less accurate indication of the behavior of the part as strain increases. This means that a part in service may deflect more than calculated from initial modulus E_0, which assumes linear relation between stress and strain. Thus, with thermoplastics under significant loadings,

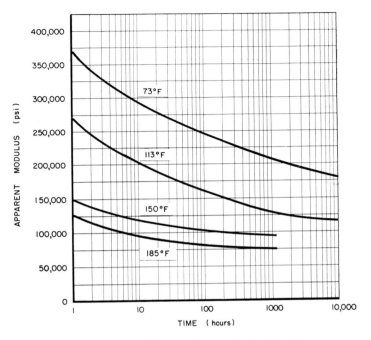

Figure 2.16. Apparent modulus *vs.* time under load and temperature for "Delrin" at 1500 psi stress.

the elastic modulus is not a "limit," as frequently termed. It becomes useful to employ the concept of "modulus accuracy limit," the value of ratio E_s/E_0 which should not be exceeded without undue creep. Experience with homogeneous plastics in a wide variety of applications shows $E_s/E_0 = .85$ to be a good value for initial design calculations. This is equivalent to designing on the basis of using 85 per cent of the initial modulus E_0. The practice is to use in design calculations the "apparent modulus" E_s as 85 per cent of the elastic modulus E_0.

Figure 2.15 plots the decreasing ratio: E_s/E_0 versus per

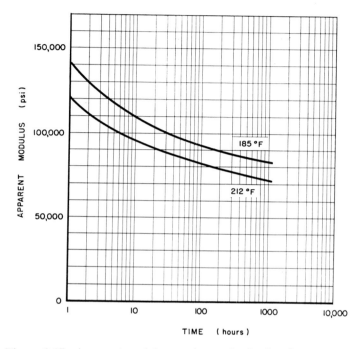

Figure 2.17. Apparent modulus *vs.* time under load and temperature for "Delrin" at 750 psi stress.

cent strain for acetal, together with standard 66 nylon and heat resistant methyl methacrylate molding compositions. From this Figure these strains and stresses at 85 per cent modulus limit can be read:

Material	Strain (%)	Stress (psi)
66 Nylon *	0.85	1400
"Delrin"	1.25	5300
Acrylic **	1.80	6900

* Conditioned to 2.5 per cent moisture content, in equilibrium at 50 per cent relative humidity.

** Methyl methacrylate, heat-resistant molding composition, ASTM Grade 8.

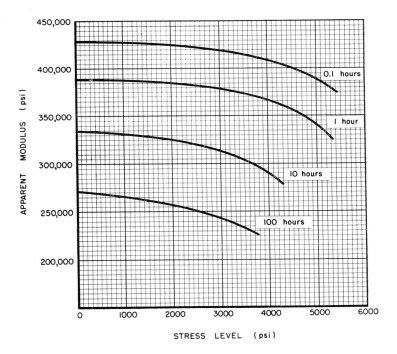

Figure 2.18. Effect of stress level on the apparent modulus (psi) of "Delrin" at different creep times—at 73°F.

Here is a problem to illustrate use of apparent modulus: A cantilever beam 4 inches long is to hold 10 pounds under continuous load for a year. The beam is in air at maximum temperature 100°F. Deflection must not exceed ⅛ inch. If rectangular beam of acetal is to be used, what are required dimensions?

Standard formula for stressed beam is

$$D = \frac{FL^3}{3EI}$$

where D = deflection; set at maximum of .125 inch
        F = force; set at 10 pounds
        L = length of beam; set at 4 inches
        E = modulus; take as 150,000 from Figure 2.16, by inter-
              polating between curves at 73°F and 113°F
        I = moment of inertia

Inserting data into above standard formula:

$$.125 = \frac{10 \times 4^3}{3 \times 150,000 \times I}$$

$$I = \frac{10 \times 4^3}{3 \times 150,000 \times .125} = 0.0114 \text{ inch}^4$$

For a rectangular section:

$$I = \frac{bd^3}{12}$$

where b = width
        d = depth, perpendicular to load

When b is set to .25 inch, then

$$I = \frac{.25d^3}{12} = 0.0114$$

$$d^3 = 0.545$$

$$d = 0.82 \text{ inch}$$

Therefore, the load will be supported by beam .25 inch wide and .82 inch deep. This should be checked to determine that the stress does not exceed that used in establishing the apparent modulus.

$$S = \frac{M}{Z}$$

where S = stress, psi
        M = bending moment
        Z = section modulus = $\frac{bd^2}{6}$

$$S = \frac{10 \times 4}{\dfrac{.25 \times .82^2}{6}} = 1440 \text{ psi, which is below the 1500 psi}$$
stress used for data of Figure 2.16.

Another example of use of structural data: Determine the bulge to be expected in aerosol bottle with flat base and cylindrical walls, stored one year with internal pressure of 100 psi. Thickness of base is 0.15 inch, and radius 0.75 inch. For this, assume stress analysis of plate with supported edges, whose deflection at center is

$$D = \frac{3pr^4(5 - 4\mu - \mu^2)}{16Eyt^3}$$

where $p =$ pressure, psi; set at 100
$r = .75$ inch
$\mu =$ Poisson's ratio, 0.38 for "Delrin"
$E_y =$ apparent modulus at one year; take as 160,000 by interpolating from Figure 2.16 for 8760 hours and 100°F
$t =$ thickness, inches; set at 0.15

$$D = \frac{3 \times 100 \times (.75)^4 \times (5 - 1.52 - .144)}{16 \times 160,000 \times (.15)^3}$$

$= .037$ inch

An actual bottle showed bulge of 0.34 inch under these conditions. When similar calculations are made for circular plate fixed at edges (unable to reduce its initial diameter) the estimated bulge is 9 mils. The actual sample is intermediate because the bottle walls behave intermediate between the two calculated cases. A bottle designed with inward bulge more than 37 mils will not likely deform under pressure to give a convex bottom which will rock.

3. PROCESSING TECHNIQUES

The major markets for acetal resin are mechanical parts. In these performance, which is of utmost importance, is governed by dimensional accuracy and stability, and uniformity of physical properties. These in large measure are determined by processing techniques used to convert molding granules into the desired shape. It follows that, more than with most plastics, the designer and user of parts of acetal resin should work closely with the molder to ensure provision of satisfactory parts. Many uses will be in replacement of metal; hence this chapter is aimed at introducing techniques for plastics processing to the design engineer who may have a limited knowledge of plastics.

Prediction of mold shrinkage, filling behavior, and dimensional stability of plastics parts is more subject to mathematical treatment than is generally realized. Such information has not been readily available, and this chapter provides more processing advice than needed by most end users. Calculations here are specific to those acetal resins which are formaldehyde homopolymers, but procedures are applicable to acetal copolymers and some other structural plastics. This treatment is not intended to be comprehensive as to mold design or operation. For that, prospective users of plastics parts should consult experienced plastics molders or suppliers of raw materials.

Plastics molding processes may be identified into five rather distinct types:

Compression Molding

Material, as molding grains or billet, is put into a mold. Heat and pressure are applied, usually by steam and hydraulic piston, to force the material to compact and fill the cavity. Figure 3.1 shows this type of molding. If the plastic is thermosetting (such as phenol-formaldehyde resin), a chemical reaction occurs, and the part may be removed without cooling the mold. If the material is thermoplastic (such

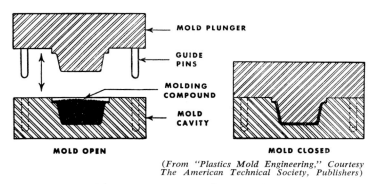

MOLD OPEN

MOLD CLOSED

(From "Plastics Mold Engineering," Courtesy The American Technical Society, Publishers)

Figure 3.1.   Compression molding.

as cellulose esters or acetal resin), essentially no chemical reaction occurs upon heating; the part is made rigid prior to removal by cooling in the mold after filling. Compression molding is rarely used for thermoplastics, because of the inherent inefficiency of alternately heating and cooling the mold. To flow and weld acetal resin it must be heated to 360°F; as its heat conductivity is low, overheating of stock at the periphery of the cavity is likely before an adequate flow temperature in center of mass is attained. Ordinarily, a mold designed for compression can be used with acetal only if it is adapted to an injection-molding machine.

Transfer Molding

A measured amount of material is heated (usually electrically) in one chamber and transferred by piston to a mold cavity of desired shape. The mold may be heated for thermoset or cooled for thermoplastic. For thermoplastics, the method rarely has advantage over injection, and is considerably more expensive. Mold cavities used for transfer molding may sometimes be adapted to injection.

Injection Molding

Material as molding granules is fed into a heating chamber. A piston or screw advances cold material to displace a measured amount of heated material into the cooled mold. Figures 3.2 and 3.3 show typical injection-molding equipment. Automatic control is usual for such factors as volume of material per shot, temperature of heating chamber, speed

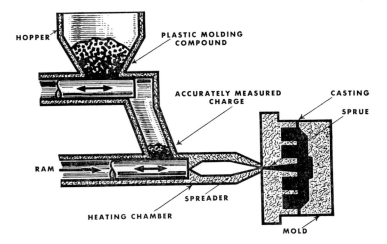

Figure. 3.2. Injection molding.

and pressure of delivery, time with mold closed and ram pressure applied, time with mold closed and ram pressure not applied, mold open to remove piece, and temperature of mold. With a properly designed mold and suitable injection machine, this process makes parts of best uniformity in size and properties. It is also the most economical for large

Figure 3.3. Injection molding machine.

quantities, and parts rarely need subsequent trimming or polishing. The bulk of this chapter will deal with injection molding of parts from acetal resin.

Except for type of feed and fluidity of hot stock, injection molding is analogous to die casting of metals. Molds built for die casting have been successfully adapted to injection-molding of acetal, although the parts will usually be of different size because of different mold shrinkage.

Extrusion

Material as molding granules is conveyed by a screw through a heated cylindrical barrel fitting close to the flight of the screw. Figure 3.12 is a diagram of the essential parts of an extruder. Plastic is heated and coalesced both by conduction from the hot barrel and by mechanical working. The die at the end of the barrel shapes the melt, delivered at controlled temperature and pressure, into continuous profile such a pipe, sheet or specific cross section. The term "extrusion molding" is occasionally used when closed cavities are filled from an extruder, which may operate continuously or intermittently.

Blow Molding

The technique of forming hollow articles, such as toys or bottles, by extruding a mass of hot plastic into a closed cavity, and introducing air by a needle to blow the mass out against the cold mold walls is called blow molding. The procedure is like that used in blowing glass containers. The melt viscosity of acetal is such that it is well adapted to this technique. Bottles made of acetal by this method are almost impermeable to essential oils and fluorinated hydrocarbon propellants used in aerosol packaging, and creep resistance under elevated temperature and pressure is excellent.

INJECTION MOLDING

The following discussion assumes that (1) reference to property data or trials with machined prototypes have shown that an acetal resin should be considered for production; (2) pieces are more complex, or are needed in such volume as to make machining uneconomic; (3) molding by injection is to be evaluated.

Acetal is not abrasive to steels ordinarily used for molds. Usual cavity, runner, and ejection systems are effective, with more care to be devoted to gates into mold cavities. Since acetals eject easily, most molds do not need high polish; acetal does, however, yield a beautiful gloss if the mold is highly polished. The question of moldability usually depends on whether the part is of a shape which is amenable to injection, and whether the part contains areas thick enough to permit filling with the acetal resin selected.

Moldability

Small parts rarely constitute a filling problem. However, where thin sections are proposed for large areas, acetal will not fill as readily as styrene or nylon, because it is less fluid and has a high freezing temperature. Factors affecting moldability are: surface area, wall thickness, distance of flow from gate to farthest point, shot weight in relation to machine capacity, speed of injection ram. Experience in a large variety of molds and injection machines is summarized in Table 3.1.

Good estimate of ability to fill can be made from calculation of flow ratio

$$\frac{AD}{T}$$

where A = total area of piece in square inches; if a box shape, it is sum of inside and outside surfaces, as each will cool the flowing plastic.

D = distance from gate to farthest point of piece, measured along path of flow, expressed in feet in order to have smaller numbers.

T = thickness in inches of the area most likely to cause difficulty. If a tapered area, use the average value of thickness; if a step area with thinnest section farthest from gate, use only the thinnest section for T.

TABLE 3.1. MOLDING DATA ON CASE HISTORIES SHOWN IN FIGURE 3.4.

Symbol	$\frac{AD}{T}$	Description of the Part	Area (sq in.)	Distance of flow (ft)	Thickness (in.)	Shot Weight (oz)	Machine Size (oz)	Cycle (sec.)
1	1630	File card box	244	.5	.075	9	16	55
2	2000	Display rack	203	.67	.068	6	12	34
3	2680	Instrument panel	240	.67	.060	19	16	155 machine was double stuffed
4	3330	Housing	445	.75	.100	12	24	45
5	3330	Washing machine agitator	400	1.25	.150	31	60	160
6	3340	Flat panel	400	.83	.100	16	32	120
7	3560	Flat panel	405	.83	.095	19	40	70
8	4960	Contoured housing	540	.92	.100	32	32	180
9	6500	Coat rack	195	2.00	.060	5	16	55
10	9100	Utility bucket	700	1.30	.100	36	16 (48 oz with a preplastifier)	217

Note: 1. In these examples, the cycles obtained are based on very short sample runs and do not necessarily represent minimum cycles that could be achieved in production. Also parts 6, 8 and 10 were molded on old, slow machines.

Flow ratio is plotted against shot weight as per cent of machine capacity in Figure 3.4. The points to the left of the dotted line are easily filled; those between the dotted and solid lines are likely to be handled best by injection machines of larger capacity or high ram speed and pressure, or by changing gating to reduce *D*. Points above the solid line should be tried only when machines of fast injection are available, or when surface imperfections may be tolerated.

Table 3.1 and Figure 3.4 justify some study, as they illustrate the effect of injection variables and are indicative of results with any thermoplastic. For instance, cases 3 and 8 show that when shot is large relative to machine capacity the cycle must be longer.

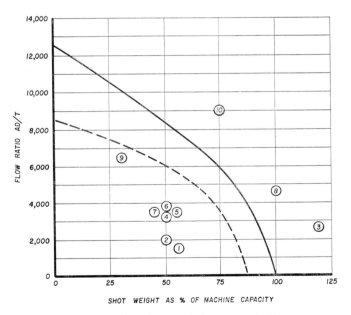

Figure 3.4. Case histories: Relative ease of filling parts.

Cycle Time

Two methods may be used for initial estimate of time of molding cycle. They are guides only, and are compared in Figure 3.5. Method A is a rule of thumb, i.e., that for sections over ¼ inch thick, the cycle should be a minute for each ¼ inch of thickness; sections up to ¼ inch may be assumed to be the same as for 66 nylon.

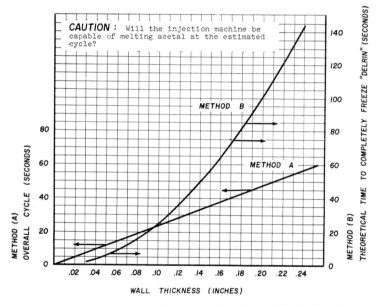

Figure 3.5. Guide to estimating cycle time. This is based on: Method A—1 min. per ¼ in. of wall thickness. Method B—theoretical time required to freeze "Delrin" completely. The surface skin becomes rigid so quickly that it is sometimes possible to eject "Delrin" even though the center of the cross section is not completely frozen. In this case, the mold cooling time would be 62% of the value shown. Add injection, ejection, and mold closing to get over-all cycle.

Note: See Figure 3.7 for melting rates.

Method B is to estimate the "fastest possible cycle," based on the cooling characteristics of acetal. Acetal can be molded on extremely fast cycles because it crystallizes and rapidly develops stiffness to permit ejection. If slight warpage or dimensional variations can be tolerated, it is frequently possible to eject thick pieces before the center is completely frozen. When ejection can be made before thorough freezing, the cooling time may be taken as $\frac{2}{3}$ of the value shown for Method B.

For any thermoplastic, the over-all molding cycle comprises: time to fill mold, cooling time, ejection time, mold closing time. Time to fill the mold with good injection equipment is indicated in Figure 3.6. To this must be added cooling time from Figure 3.5. Ejection and mold closing time must also be added to obtain the total cycle; they are usually functions only of the injection machine, but if molds have side-pull components or require placing inserts, added allowance should be made.

Method B projects a minimum cycle based only on the cooling rate of acetal. For the specific machine considered, it should now be determined whether this minimum cycle permits adequate plastifying of material. Too rapid cycling delivers a melt of nonhomogeneous fluidity and temperature, and may actually provide incompletely filled shots. Melting rates for typical machines are shown in Figure 3.7. Points spotted on that Figure are explained in Table 3.2.

Number of Cavities

This is often critical to success, and it is remarkable how rarely a detailed mathematical basis is used to reach the decision. Factors to consider are: (1) economics of tooling; (2) shot capacity of machine; (3) clamping capacity of machine; (4) melting rate of machine; (5) hold-up time in heating cylinder.

Acetal Resins

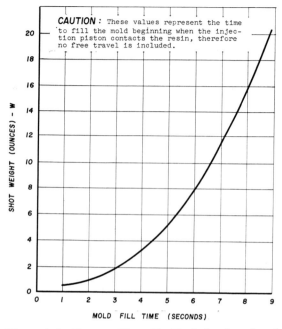

Figure 3.6. Time to fill mold. Typical values based on good injection equipment.

Economics. Increasing the number of cavities usually decreases the production costs, at least up to point where much larger machine is indicated. Increasing the number of cavities also increases initial cost of mold and its maintenance; it may also make too many pieces for the machine operator to handle economically if trimming is to be done while subsequent shots are being molded. An approximate curve can be drawn of decreasing cost of production as the number of cavities is increased. On the same graph the increasing cost of mold can be plotted versus number of cavities. The sum of these curves is plotted as a third line; it will

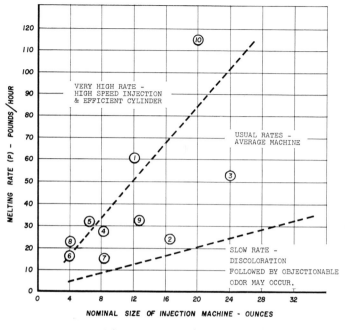

Figure 3.7. Melting rates.

show a dip at number of cavities *N,* where sum of tooling
and production is least, or it may show very little added saving
with increase beyond a certain number of cavities. Normally,
an end user should provide the fullest information as to production requirements, and let the molder determine the number of cavities and choice of injection machine. The optimum
economic number of cavities may be too great for proposed
molding equipment.

Shot Capacity of Machine. This can be estimated from

$$N_1 = \frac{.75M - W_r}{W_p}$$

TABLE 3.2. MOLDING DATA ON CASE HISTORIES SHOWN IN
FIGURE 3.7—MELTING RATES.

Symbol	No. of Cavities	Wall Thickness (in.)	Shot Weight (oz)	Machine Size (oz)	Melting Rate (lb/hr)
1	1	.080	6.5	12	61
2	1	.060	5.5	16	22
3	1	.100	10	24	52
4	2	.100	3	8	28
5	3	.060	3	8	32
6	4	.060	2	4	18
7	4	.125	6	8	15
8	8	.050	1	4	21
9	12	.250	6	12	31
10	16	.080	11	20	115

Note: Runs 1 and 10 were made on new, fast injecting machines capable of very fast cycles and high melt rates.

where N_1 = maximum cavities on shot basis
M = machine capacity, name plate rating in ounces
W_r = weight of sprue and runner, in ounces
W_p = weight of single part

When flow ratio $\frac{(AD)}{T}$ exceeds 2,000, shot capacity is better estimated as

$$N_1 = \frac{.50M - W_r}{W_p}$$

Clamping Capacity. The ability of machine to hold the mold together against the force of incoming plastics may limit the number of cavities, particularly when molding thin flat pieces. Estimate may be made from

$$N_2 = \frac{F/5 - A_r}{A_p}$$

where N_2 = maximum cavities on clamp basis
F = clamp capacity, in tons
A_r = projected area of sprue and runner, in square inches
A_p = projected area of molded part

Melting Rate of Injection Cylinder. This is important in relation to the number of cavities, and may be estimated from:

$$N_3 = \frac{PC/225 - W_r}{W_p}$$

where N_3 = maximum cavities on melting basis
  P = plastifying or melting rate in pounds per hour (Figure 3.7 is guide)
  C = overall cycle in seconds
  W_r = weight of sprue and runners, in ounces
  W_p = weight of molded part, in ounces

Hold-up Time. This is the time that material is in heating cylinder. Calculations (a) through (d) above have been used to determine whether the number of cavities considered for the mold is within capacity of proposed machine. Calculation of hold-up time is the reverse, to determine whether the capacity of the machine is so much larger than the requirements of cycle and proposed mold that there may be problems introduced by thermal degradation of the polymer. This estimate may be made by the following calculation:

$$H = \frac{M \times I}{S} \times \frac{C}{60}$$

where H = hold-up time in minutes
  M = name plate capacity of machine, in ounces
  S = shot weight, including pieces, sprue and runner, in ounces
  C = cycle time in seconds
  I = inventory factor, the number of shots of name plate capacity contained in cylinder. This is usually about 6; that is, an 8-ounce injection cylinder will contain 48 ounces of material

The result should be checked against Figure 3.8 which shows average experience of a number of machines. Parts molded above the dotted line may show yellow streaking or surface imperfections. Parts molded above the solid line

Acetal Resins

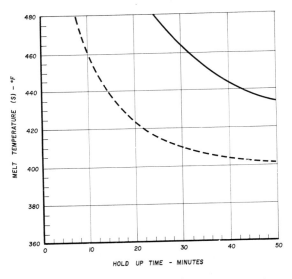

Figure 3.8. Limits of hold up time *vs.* temperature.

are quite sure to have discoloration and surface defects, and possible porosity in sections above ¼ inch thick. Production will be satisfactory if H is up to 15 minutes and questionable if it is above 35 minutes.

Final selection of number of cavities is to be made by comparing numbers from each of above estimates. If N_1, N_2 or N_3 is smaller than the "economical" number N, it is advisable to decrease the number of cavities or use a different (usually larger) machine. Or if H exceeds 30 minutes where good surface is needed, use a smaller machine.

Mold Design

The preceding discussion has defined the number of cavities to be provided. Acetal has been successfully molded in almost every type of injection mold currently used: three-plate, tunnel-gated, hot runner, valve-gated, family, 200-cavity, and multiple side pull. No special design is needed for this material, but more attention to construction details may be necessary for top performance.

Materials of Construction. Mold steels usually employed are satisfactory, as in normal experience acetal is neither corrosive nor abrasive to molds. Prolonged use in very hot molds may reduce polish in areas of fastest flow. Chrome plating or a hard stainless steel may in such rare cases be preferable. If especially rapid cooling is desired to take advantage of rapid setting rate of acetal, cavities may be made of beryllium-copper alloy. These alloys should not be used for hot-runner or valve gating portions of mold because copper catalyzes decomposition of hot acetal and causes yellow streaking. High polish is needed in the mold only where molded parts are to be glossy. Even in three-plate molds, acetal ejects easily from unpolished runners.

Coring. Coring is the provision of channels within the mold to provide for circulating fluid to maintain temperature. As many parts of acetal will mate with other parts, coring should be such that all cavity surfaces have the same access to the temperature-controlling fluid. If the mold is for a part requiring high gloss over large area, it may be operated from 220° to 250°F. When a large volume of resin is injected, mold areas near the gate may get too hot, and the circulating fluid may also be required to cool these areas as well as to heat the cavities. While separate coring channels may be employed for gates and for cavities, it is usually preferable to modify the gates. Changing to a fan or flash gate will usually distribute the heat so that uniform mold temperature is attainable with a single coring system. For most molding, adequate surface appearance will be achieved with the mold at 150 to 170°F.

Design of Cavity. Cavity design is primarily concerned with establishing size so that the parts molded will be within specified dimensions. Table 3.3 lists a variety of mold shrinkage data. Figure 3.9 is based on the same data and added experience; it shows the relation between average mold shrinkage (except in direction of mold opening) and two variables: thickness of part and gate area. Effects may be noted for variation in gate thickness, gate land length, pressure in mold, ram speed, and flow orientation. These effects are minor, and should be ignored in initial cavity design unless experience in similar parts provides some guidance.

Figure 3.9 is based on experience with gates of various

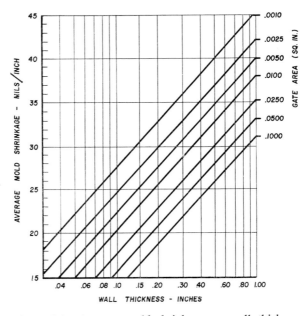

Figure 3.9. Average mold shrinkage *vs.* wall thickness of the part and gate area.

TABLE 3.3. MOLD SHRINKAGE DATA.

Example	Shape	Cavity Dimensions (in.)	Mold Shrinkage (mils/in.)	Mold Temperature (°F)
1	Gear gate, area = 0.0061 in.²	Dia. 1.87	30	80
			29	140
			30	200
			32	265
		Thickness 0.81	27	80
			27	140
			25	200
			22	265
		Core (for hub) 0.50	20	80
			23	140
			23	200
			23	265
2	Tensile Test Bar end gate, area = 0.0035 in.²	Length 5.01	23	80
			23	140
			24	200
			25	265
		Width 0.750	22	80
			22	140
			23	200
			23	265
		Thickness 0.126	3	80
			5	140
			8	200
			8	265
3	Tensile Test Bar end gate, area = 0.0035 in.²	Length 5.01	30	80
			32	140
			32	200
			31	265
		Width 0.750	32	80
			32	140
			29	200
			28	265
		Thickness 0.250	14	80
			17	140
			17	200
			17	265

55

Table 3.3b. Mold Shrinkage Data.

Example	Shape	Cavity Dimensions (in.)	Mold Shrinkage (mils/in.)	Mold Temperature (°F)
4	Disc edge gate, area = 0.023 in.^{2}	Dia. 3.38	13	80
			13	140
			15	200
			19	265
		Thickness 0.142	1	80
			4	140
			13	200
				265
5	Disc edge gate, area = 0.023 in.^{2}	Dia. 3.38	22	80
			23	140
			24	200
		Thickness 0.252	11	80
			49	140
			68	200
6	Tensile Test Bar center gate, area = 0.0018 in.^{2}	Length 5.01	23	80
			23	140
			24	200
			25	265
		Width 0.750	24	80
			24	140
			25	200
			26	265
		Thickness 0.126	0	80
			2	140
			4	200
			6	265
7	Tensile Test Bar center gate, area = 0.0018 in.^{2}	Length 5.01	31	80
			32	140
			31	200
			30	265
		Width 0.750	31	80
			33	140
			28	200
			26	265
		Thickness 0.250	18	80
			20	140
			18	200
			17	265

56

TABLE 3.3c. MOLD SHRINKAGE DATA.

Example	Shape	Cavity Dimensions (in.)	Mold Shrinkage (mils/in.)	Mold Temperature (°F)
8	Disc edge gate, area $= 0.006$ in.^{2}	Dia. 2.25	26 29 29 30	80 140 200 265
		Thickness 0.147	6 13 43 47	80 140 200 265
9	Disc edge gate, area $= 0.023$ in.^{2}	Dia. 2.25	16 18 20 22	80 140 200 265
		Thickness 0.147	3.4 0.0 2.0 7.0	80 140 200 265
10	Disc edge gate, area $= 0.059$ in.^{2}	Dia. 4.02	13 18	80 140
		Thickness 0.147	55 80	80 140
11	Disc edge gate, area $= 0.059$ in.^{2}	Dia. 4.02	18 19 22 24	80 140 200 265
		Thickness 0.267	45 41 27 34	80 140 200 265
12	Disc edge gate, area $= 0.059$ in.^{2}	Dia. 4.02	22 21 23	80 140 200
		Thickness 0.370	19 32 25	80 140 200
13	Sleeve Bearing gate, area $= 0.0078$ in.^{2}	Length 1.010	18	150
		I.D. $= 1.030$	14	150

57

cross sections. Data do not apply to dimensions in direction of mold opening, because such dimensions vary with the clamping force; in that direction, mold shrinkage is usually half or less than the shrinkage perpendicular to direction of mold opening. As an example of use of this figure, assume wall thickness of 0.100 inch, and gate .05 × .05 inch. Starting at 0.10 thickness, read up to .0025 square inch gate area, then left to average mold shrinkage of 24 mils per inch.

Parts to be molded to very close tolerances require stepwise approach to sizing of cavity, considering actual mold shrinkage, shrinkage due to annealing, and dimensional changes due to environmental temperature and humidity. Usual commercial molding practice delivers tolerance in acetal of ±.003 inch per inch for first inch and ±.002 inch per inch for subsequent inches. Precision molding with precise machine controls has delivered parts ±.002 for the first inch and less than .001 inch for subsequent inches.

Users should not specify tolerances for plastics parts so fine as in metals until the need has been demonstrated. Closer tolerances are more expensive. Because of the resilience of acetal, tolerances larger than with similar metal parts have provided quiet operation and absence of backlash.

For very close tolerances, a trial cavity should be made and mounted in mold so as to be fed with a runner system such as proposed for production mold. The trial cavity should be sized from data of Table 3.3 and Figure 3.9, adjusted for humidity changes from Figure 2.7 (p. 21) and adjusted for annealing from Table 3.4. A practical value for annealing shrinkage is .002 inch per inch for external part dimension and .005 inch per inch for internal dimensions.

Design of Gates, Runners and Sprue. Design of these parts is quite important for acetal because of its rapid freezing rate and inability to pack the cavity once the gate has cooled and sealed.

TABLE 3.4. ENVIRONMENTAL SHRINKAGE OF ACETAL RESIN DUE TO STRESS RELAXATION.

(Parts were tested until shrinkage stopped)

Environmental temperature	Shrinkage (mils/in.)
Routine Molding. Samples annealed at 320°F for 15 minutes	
—40 to 170°F	<0.5
170 to 212°F	≦1.5
212 to 248°F	≦2.5
Molded With Mold Temperature of 250°F. No annealing treatment	
—40 to 170°F	<0.5
180°F	1
200°F	2.5
212°F	4
Routine Molding—Cold mold (100°F-150°F). No annealing treatment	
—40 to 125°F	≦1
125 to 150°F	≦1.5
150 to 175°F	≦3

Note: The shrinkage values were based on measurements of the pieces made at room temperature after exposure as indicated. The above results were obtained on various parts as described below. Corroborative data should be obtained on other shapes to ensure maximum precision.

	Soap dish:	4″ x 3″ x 1″ deep—.070″ wall thickness
	Gear:	2″ Dia. x 1″ thick
Description of	Sphere:	approximately 1″ Dia.
parts measured	Dumbbell tensile bars:	5″ long x .125″ thick
		5″ long x .25″ thick
	Fatigue bars:	4″ x 2″ x .25″
	Discs:	2″ Dia. x .125″ thick
		3″ Dia. x .125″, .25″, and .365″ thick
		4″ Dia. x .125″, .25″, and .365″ thick

The gate should be designed to:

(1) facilitate separation of molded part from runner; this reduces finishing costs and is essential for automatic molding;

(2) seal edge of cavity, permitting fast ejection even when part is not completely frozen;

(3) keep residual stress in part at minimum, by preventing packing of continuing application of ram during freezing portion of cycle;

(4) provide equal back pressure in all runners, facilitating speedy filling and equal weight among similar cavities.

General recommendations on locating gates:

(1) avoid locating where part may be flexed, as residual stress is greater at gate and part may distort or break;

(2) avoid locating gate where weld lines will be put in area requiring flexing;

(3) put gate where its removal by clipping or breaking will give good enough finish;

(4) direct flow into cavity against wall, so as to avoid surface marks from puddling into cavity;

(5) for thin sections, gate in direction of longest dimension to fill;

(6) if part is molded around core pin, avoid gating which would shift core pin; high fluidity of acetal readily transfers force of injection ram into cavity;

(7) gate so that entering plastic will sweep air out to parting line or ejector pin.

The type of gate should be chosen in consideration of the geometry of the part. A flat rectangular gate serves for most cavities, and is easiest to machine and most economical of material. It should be flared at entrance to cavity.

Fan gates are preferred for large thin sections, particularly with flow ratios above 500:1. Fan gates have faster delivery rates. They are simply broad entry paths, and may taper to a thin section of the part from a runner several times as thick as the part.

Flash gates are essentially runners going along the part cavity, with a narrow wall separating them. They provide large area for flow, short gate-seal time, and frequently permit such a thin channel into the cavity that parts can be separated from gate and runner with no subsequent finishing to provide clean parts.

Full-round gates are easily milled into the mold and provide rapid delivery of material. Their disadvantage is that they do not permit increasing area for filling without increasing gate-seal time.

Tab gates are used where surface finish is of utmost importance. A tab gate enters the cavity through an extension to the cavity; usually it has less area than the tab entry into cavity, and thus seals off the tab and part. Tab gating is used to smooth and apportion flow into multicavity molds. It is always positioned at a right angle to flow into the part so as to avoid jetting of molten material into cavity.

Diaphragm gates are used when a part is cylindrical and the wall is so thin that required injection pressure might shift the core if it is not applied uniformly. The diaphragm gate is a web across the core, usually providing entry of material radially to the cylindrical cavity. Removal usually requires a finishing operation.

Ring gates accomplish the objective of diaphragm gates, sometimes with lower cost for mold and removal of gate. The incoming plastic is admitted to annular space around the part cavity, and flow is then fairly uniform down the core pin. Weld lines are unavoidable opposite the point of entry of plastic into annular channel.

Gate dimensions are particularly important with acetal because many parts are required to be dimensionally accurate and because the material sets rapidly. The land (length of gate measured in direction of material flow) should be as short as possible, while retaining enough metal for strength in the mold. Generally the land is half the diameter of the runner; for rectangular gates a start may be at .04 inch length, shortening if need arises for more rapid filling. Flash-gated molds have worked well with lands less than .015 inch. Close tolerance molding in multicavity molds requires that all identical cavities have lands of uniform length in order to provide equal pressure into each cavity. Gate diameter should rarely be less than .035 inch, or equivalent cross-section for other than round gates. Gates too small may require boosting temperature or pressure of injection to levels causing discoloration or surface defects. Gates that are too large may require unnecessarily long molding cycles in order to seal against back flow in gate. Gate seal time should be less than 80 per cent of estimated molding cycle. Figure 3.10 plots average gate-seal time versus mold temperature for several gate diameters.

The runner which leads acetal to various cavities should be of the same general dimensions and patterns as for other thermoplastics. Round runners are preferred because they provide minimum ratio of area to volume, and thus deliver material of higher and more uniform temperature. The usual practice is to have the runner about the thickness of the heaviest section of the part. The runner should not be less than .060 inch nor more than .40 inch diameter, although larger diameter may be required for very long runners. Runners need not be polished, either for speed of delivery or ease of ejection.

The sprue bushing is the adaptor, usually recessed into one plate of mold, which mates with the nozzle of the injection machine and admits plastic to the runners. It tapers from minimum at point of nozzle contact in order to pull

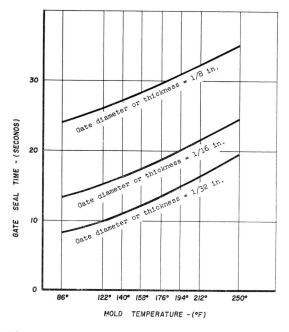

Figure 3.10. Gate seal time *vs.* gate size and mold temperature.

Note: Data obtained on a full-round gate. However, the smallest cross-sectional dimension of any other type of gate can be used to estimate gate seal time.

all plastic with shot up to where nozzle maintains inventory for next shot. The downstream end should be at least as large as main runner to ensure that plastic does not freeze at that point before the gates seal. Standard taper is 2.5° included angle, although acetal and other plastics will usually benefit from a 3.5° taper. Bushings longer than 4 inches should be recessed into the mold plate, and the nozzle lengthened to match. This is to economize material, permit wider angle of taper, and to provide better temperature control.

Ejection and Venting Practices. Acetal does not stick to molds, and rapidly develops the stiffness necessary for ejection. Where ejection of thick parts is contemplated before the center has fully solidified, ejector pins should be carefully considered as to size, number and location. Warpage may result when large areas are pushed from the cavity with ejector pins spaced too widely. Standard practice is quite satisfactory, and the plastic material has usually hardened enough to prevent marring of the surface.

Venting of the cavity to permit escape of air is advisable to allow more rapid fill of the cavity and the short cycles possible for thin sections. Standard practice of channels .002 x .025 inch leading from the cavity to the outer mold face is satisfactory. Rapid setting of acetal usually gives less evidence of flash with such vents than with 66 nylon or general-purpose polystyrene.

Precision Parts. These require conformance to a chosen dimension, uniformity of dimension, or stability of dimension under time and environment, all of which are influenced by pressure in the mold. Pressure in the cavity (determined by strain gauge on ejector pin) falls off as the plastic solidifies, although the hydraulic system of the injection machine maintains uniform pressure on the ram. This means that the same mold in two different machines may produce parts of different size. To ensure that molding conditions are similar when the mold is reinstalled in the same or a different machine, it may be profitable to incorporate in the mold a cavity, say, .25 x .035 x 5 inches long. Machine conditions for most uniform parts will then be those which give the same length of fill in this strip.

Choice of Injection Machine

This is not usually critical except for precision parts. So long as unmelted particles are not delivered to cavity, higher ram pressures and speeds are preferable, which usually indicate a newer machine. Hold-up time is critical and may dictate use of smaller heating cylinder than that of optimum cycle. Recommendations on hold-up time (Figure 3.8) are valid only when the melt temperature is determined by using mold cycle to shoot into air over thermocouple.

Temperature uniformity can be improved by inserting a variable transformer in line with the heater band, reducing fluctuations due to cycling of controller. Improved uniformity will also result from use of dual thermocouples in parallel, one near the heating surface and the other deep within the cylinder wall. Dual thermocouples provide better control and are usually less expensive than adding another controlled heater band.

Operating Procedures

Operating procedures for the injection molding of acetal are not greatly different from those with other thermoplastics, once it is realized that the viscosity of the molten resin does not change much within the tolerable temperature range. The viscosity of injection-grade acetal is comparable to that of typical low-density polyethylene, and the viscosity of extrusion-grade is comparable to that of standard heat-resistant methacrylate. Neither grade of acetal changes viscosity with temperature as much as polyethylene or methacrylate. Normally, acetal from either series is molded from 400 to 440°F, and raising cylinder temperature does not markedly increase the flow. When more flow is necessary, it is usually best achieved by enlarging runners or gates.

Stabilization of Dimensions after Molding

This may occasionally be a necessary step. Because of high deformation temperature, low moisture absorption and low creep, acetal resins have a degree of dimensional stability unusual among injectable plastics. However, as with metals and other plastics, moldings of acetal may have stressed portions as a result of molding conditions. Release of these stresses with time, elevated temperature or applied loadings can result in dimensional changes which are called environmental shrinkage.

Hot molds will produce moldings having least stress. Further reduction may require annealing. Table 3.4 gives environmental shrinkage for various mold temperatures, with and without annealing; data are average for a variety of molded shapes.

Annealing should be in the absence of air, to prevent discoloration. It is preferably performed in refined mineral oil; automotive motor oil is satisfactory if it does not contain additives such as phosphates which may be absorbed by the plastic.

Recommended annealing temperature for parts up to an inch thick is 320°F. Temperatures above 325°F may cause deterioration of physical properties or warpage. Average part thickness may be used to determine annealing time. Figure 3.11 suggests annealing times for various thicknesses.

Parts greater than an inch thick will usually have enough molded-in stress to make lower temperature advisable for annealing to avoid warpage; 300°F for an hour for each inch of thickness has been found quite satisfactory.

Pieces should be cooled slowly upon removal from annealing bath in order to preclude new stresses due to more rapid cooling of the outer portion.

Use of Acetals in Molds made for Die-Casting Metals

Molds initially made for die casting of zinc, magnesium or aluminum may be used in injection molding equipment for molding acetal resins. Largely because of higher coefficient

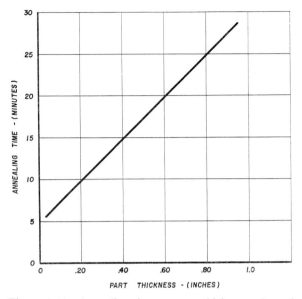

Figure 3.11. Annealing time *vs.* part thickness. Annealing temperature $= 320 \pm 3°F$.

of thermal contraction, parts of acetal will be smaller than metal parts from the same mold. Zinc alloy parts are usually .005 inch per inch smaller than the cavity (both measured at room temperature). Aluminum parts are .01 inch per inch smaller, and acetal parts .02 inch per inch smaller. Design of plastics molding equipment differs from die casting practice, and retooling of sprue bushing, locating ring, and gates may require changes for production.

EXTRUSION

Acetal resin has been commercially extruded into sheet, rod, tube and shaped profiles. It has also been extruded onto wire, and made into blow-molded bottles, where the mold is fed with extruded tubing. A schematic of usual plastics extruder is in Figure 3.12. Special designs or materials of construction are not needed in extrusion equipment. Some elements of good general extrusion practice may become more important because of the relatively sharp melting and freezing points of acetal resin, and the need to avoid local overheating.

Extrusion melt temperature is usually 390 to 420°F. The ratio of barrel length to diameter should be 20:1 or more, to provide greater heat transfer without need for high barrel temperatures, and to give better melt uniformity. The barrel should have three or four heat zones, controlled independently. A thermocouple to measure stock temperature is advisable. A metering type screw is distinctly preferable to minimize delivery of unmelted particles to the screen pack or die.

Acetal resin is provided in a higher-viscosity grade that is better suited for extrusion than the standard injection-molding grade. At 400°F, the melt viscosity of low-density

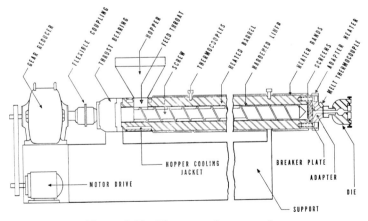

Figure 3.12. Elements of an extruder.

polyethylene of melt index 3 is about midway between the extrusion and molding grades of acetal resin. Over the operating range 380 to 420°F, the viscosity of acetal resin changes less than that of low-density polyethylene, and considerably less than that of methacrylate molding composition in its molding range. Although the melt of acetal is as viscous as that of other extrusion resins, it has low "melt elasticity." This means that the melt will quickly lose shape, and rapid quenching of extrudate is usually practiced in order to hold the form.

Thermal degradation causes gassing, with attendant surface blemishes or voids in thick sections. It may or may not be preceded by discoloration. Rigorous streamlining of extruder and die sections is essential. Seals should be tight between barrel and breaker plate, adaptor and die sections. Copper or brass parts should not be in contact with hot resin, as copper accelerates discoloration of the resin.

In starting to extrude acetal resins, a clean machine should be used; or preceding material must be purged with low melt index polyethylene. Similarly, in changing from acetal to another resin, and intermediate purge with polyethylene is recommended to reduce gassing due either to the temperature needed to melt the other material, or to chemical interaction with acidic materials such as vinyl chloride. The decomposition products—almost entirely formaldehyde—are irritating but not toxic in the amounts which can be endured for a few minutes. In the event of severe overheating, the extrudate can be dumped into cold water.

Tube is made by conventional free extrusion into water bath. Air gap between die and bath level is 1 to 3 inches. Dies may be cross-head or straight-through. Draw-down ratio (area ratio of cross section at die to cross-section of desired product) may be from 4:1 to 10:1.

Sheet is made with a conventional three-roll finisher to impart surface gloss. Roll temperatures may be as high as 260°F for good surface. Because of the quick-setting nature of acetal resin, the caliper must be determined by die adjustments, not at the rolls. It is desirable to have die jaws extend well into the nip of the rolls.

Shapes are made through streamlined dies, usually feeding directly into the end of a cooling trough supplied with a rubber dam which conforms to the shape desired.

Wire-coating is done by a tubing die with vacuum. On fine wire draw-down ratio may be as high as 40 to 1. Wire speeds in excess of 1,800 feet per minute have been used.

Rod is extruded with a long cooling die. The major problem is voids in center, due to high shrinkage when acetal resin goes from liquid to semicrystalline state. A brake is usually needed to restrain the motion of the rod and to permit extrudate to pack the center during cooling.

FABRICATION

Following the practice of the plastics industry, "fabrication" includes the operations of cutting, polishing, fastening and decorating, as opposed to "processing," which means the operations of molding and extrusion.

Machining of acetal resins may be carried out on standard shop equipment for sawing, milling and drilling. These operations are usually more easily accomplished than with soft brass or aluminum. In most cases, the final cut should be at least .002 inch, as the material is resilient enough to deflect under lesser cuts. Fine shavings should not be allowed to accumulate because of fire hazard, although rapid cuts may be taken without fear of generating enough heat to ignite the work. It is seldom advisable to use cutting oils or water to aid in machining. Wet band sanding is recommended to reduce dust and work temperature. For best dimensional stability, large stock should be annealed prior to machining. If the part is large, it may be rough-machined, then reannealed before final machining. Massive pieces should never be cut without first annealing, as the outer skin may be under tension from thermal contraction of the casting or extrusion process. Cutting a highly stressed skin may lead to violent rupture of the piece.

Blanking. Small flat parts such as washers, grommets and non-precision gears $\frac{1}{16}$ inch or less in thickness can be produced economically by blanking or stamping from sheet stock. Conventional dies are used. If cracking occurs on thicker sheet, it may be helpful to preheat the sheet.

Drilling. Standard twist drills may be used. Drills for cutting plastics or soft brass may cause overheating in deep holes. When drilling is done at high speed, coolant water or cutting oil is desirable to prevent overheating; this cooling will provide smoother holes and prevent holes from becoming undersized upon thermal contraction of thin walls.

Finishing. Power-driven rotary steel burrs at high speeds are effective in model making or in removing flash from prototype moldings. Coarse abrasive discs are good on high-speed hand grinders. Very effective is a mill file with deep, single-cut, coarse, curved teeth, known as a vixen file.

Milling. Standard milling machines and cutters may be used. End mills should preferably be single-fluted, because the greater chip clearance generates less frictional heat.

Polishing. Very high polish can be applied by usual ashing, polishing, and wiping procedures. Ashing is done with ventilated fabric wheel, of alternating 6 and 12 inch muslin discs. This wheel is kept dressed by slurry of pumice and water while buffing. Acetal should be held lightly against the wheel and constantly moved to prevent local cutting or discoloration. Speed of the wheel should be about 1,000 rpm.

Polishing is easily done on a wheel of muslin discs, alternately 6 and 12 inch diameter. This wheel is operated dry, with polishing compound applied to half its width. The other half is untreated, and is used to wipe off polishing compound. Optimum speeds for 12-inch wheel range from 1,000 to 1,500 rpm.

Reaming. Hand or collar reamers are effective. Reamers should not be advanced too slowly as the heat generated may lead to stretching rather than cutting hole to size. Subsequent cooling may give an undersized hole if the part is thin. If the part is so thick that temperature rise is confined to the hole surface, reaming may leave an oversized hole upon cooling.

Sanding. Wet belt or disc sanding is effective; high polish is subsequently attained by simple buffing.

Sawing. Band saws, jig saws and table saws can be used without modification. Speed of saw or feed is not critical. Saw blades should have some set as tooth clearance is needed to prevent melting the plastic.

Shaping. Standard shapers and tools are very effective, and no change is recommended.

Tapping, threading. Conventional equipment is satisfactory. Lubricant or coolant is needed only at very high speeds or for deep holes. It may be desirable to use tap .005 inch oversize because acetal is more resilient than metals and if the wall surrounding the hole is not thick, the plastic will expand. Upon removal of tap, the material springs back and the thread is slightly too small. Where screws are inserted into drilled or molded hole, thread-cutting rather than thread-forming screws have shown higher pull-out strengths.

Turning. Standard metal-working lathes are preferred; wood-working lathes may be too slow for smooth cuts; tools should be ground as for free-cutting brass. Standard chipbreakers are recommended although not used for most plastics. Back rake is preferred to eliminate drag. Where length of work is long and diameter is small, steady rests will be needed to reduce deflection. They may require a coolant if velocity is high or duration of turning is long.

Assembly of Parts

Assembly of acetal to itself, other plastics or metals can be done mechanically by screws or rivets because of its good resistance to creep. A limited variety of adhesives give fair bonds, but solvent cements are relatively ineffective. Copolymeric acetal resins will permit better attack by solvent adhesives. Epoxy and resorcinol resins give joints of moderate strength in shear, but usually peel in torsion. Best results have been obtained from sanded surfaces and rubber- or polyester-based adhesives cured above 200°F. Shear strengths of lap joints around 500 psi have been obtained. Acid or alkali etch of acetal resins promotes adhesion, but parts should be fully rinsed to avoid attack or irregular cure of adhesive. In general, acetal can be bonded well to itself only by welding.

Hot-plate Welding. In this technique, the two surfaces to be joined are placed against a hot plate to melt them, and are then pressed together. Plate should be 450 to 550°F. For large areas, 10 minutes may be needed against plate at 450°F, while 1-inch pipe is readily welded after 20 seconds at 550°F. Strengths up to 9,000 psi (90 per cent of material strength) are attained. Pressure should be only enough to assure contact with heating surface, and with matching part of acetal. Flash more than $\frac{1}{16}$ inch from the joint indicates excessive pressure.

Aluminum hot plates are recommended because of uniform temperature. Copper and brass should not be used because of catalytic decomposition of the resin. Thermostatic control of the heating surface is highly desirable. Small areas will be ready to use in several minutes. Cooling by a blast of air or liquid quench should not be practiced because of unbalanced stresses imposed by nonuniform cooling of periphery of joint.

Hot-gas Welding. This method may be preferred to hot plates for large pieces, and also permits rigid alignment of pieces in jigs. It consumes more time and requires a high degree of operator skill. Tensile strengths of 6,000 psi have been obtained with ³⁄₆₄-inch welding rod of acetal and air at 575°F ¼ inch from the gun nozzle. A weld of 7,500 psi has been obtained using nitrogen at 630°F. The nitrogen operation is faster, and without danger of discoloring or igniting the resin.

Hot-Wire Welding. This method clamps a wire between two pieces of acetal, then applies electric current to heat wire and melt adjacent plastic. Pieces are lightly pressed together to form a weld. The method is usually free of flash, quick, and applicable to complex lines. Shear strength of 750 pounds per inch of embedded wire can be obtained. Molded parts to be so assembled may have a retaining groove molded for the wire.

Induction Welding. A metallic insert can be heated by induction to make joints similar to those of hot wire welding. The method lends itself to automatic operations and is fast. Use of a perforated ring permits acetal to flow through and make a strong joint.

Spin Welding. This unique and efficient method assembles thermoplastics with circular joints. One section is rotated at high speed against a stationary piece and frictional heat quickly melts the contacting surfaces. When the relative motion is suddenly stopped, the melt solidifies to a weld that is nearly as strong as the parent material. The operation requires about a second for rotation, and satisfactory conditions of timing, presure and rotational speed are determined with only a few trials. The usual set-up is a jig to hold the bottom piece and a drill press to hold and rotate a mating piece. The jig can quickly release the lower portion once the weld is made, and the drill press slowed and welded assembly removed. Alternatively, the pieces may be placed in contact, the lower one being kept from rotating; as with a rubber driving ring, the drill press rotates the upper piece by friction. Raising the drill press instantly releases the top of the assembly, and the weld freezes.

Spin welding is an effective and economical technique for joining two halves of a bottle, permitting different colors for the body or a contrasting shoulder area. The joint is leakproof. It is also self-cleaning, so that cap or dispensing head may usually be welded to a freshly filled bottle without removing spilled contents from the interface to be sealed.

Decorating and Finishing

Acetal resins can be finished by the several techniques common to plastics: painting, printing, hot stamping, and vacuum metallizing. Solvent resistance of polymers which are primarily all of formaldehyde is such that special priming techniques are usually needed. Copolymers with other aldehydes are somewhat more readily attacked by coating solvents, and for some uses may not require special priming techniques.

Painting. Painting has been done on large scale, automobile instrument clusters being a good example. The usual technique is to flow or spray with primer especially prepared for acetal resin, followed by baking above 200°F. The top coat is then standard acrylic, alkyd or cellulose nitrate paint. Adhesion is good under humidity, and by the usual peel test with pressure-sensitive tape after knife-scoring. Instead of the primer-paint coat, adhesion may be gained by acid-etching the acetal part. This is conveniently done by hydrochloric, phosphoric or sulfonic acid and modifying agents in chlorinated solvent in regular degreasing equipment. Painting can then be a one-coat system. Acid-etching must be carefully done to avoid cracking along lines of molded-in stress. Surface at gate and weld line must be controlled in molding in order to get uniform "satinizing" of surface when the desire is to apply but a single topcoat.

Printing. Requirements for adhesion and uniformity of appearance are not usually so extreme for printing as for painting, and primers are not customary. Commercial printing inks provide good adhesion, but only when baked around 250°F to obtain adhesion and resistance to abrasion.

Hot Stamping. Commercial stamping tapes work well, although not all compositions are satisfactory. Suppliers of hot-stamping tapes should be advised that use on acetal resins is intended.

Vacuum Metallizing. Bright metallic finishes are obtained with standard techniques. Acetal surface is primed with same primer as used before painting, then baked to remove volatiles. This is followed by usual metallizing base coat, vacuum metallizing, and clear topcoat.

Coating with Acetal Resins

Coatings are usually employed to provide chemical or weathering resistance. As the acetal resins are not recommended for resistance to strong acid or alkali, there has been little work done on coating techniques. One area of utility is in provision of surfaces resistant to abrasion, or for bearings.

Two techniques have been employed: fluidized bed coating of hot substrate, and solvent or dispersion coatings followed by heating to coalesce. Metal parts may be oven-heated to 370°F, then immersed in acetal resin ground to less than 50 mesh, fluidized by stream of nitrogen or carbon dioxide. Air or oxygen are not recommended unless discoloration or embrittlement of the resin can be tolerated. The hot part is held in agitated resin bath a few seconds, then post-fused in oven at 360 to 370°F for 10 to 15 minutes. Carried out twice, this process will provide coating up to .010 inch thick. Quenching coated article in cold water will provide better gloss and toughness. Induction heating of metal part, and post-fusing by induction work well and provide better uniformity. Usually, a better surface and toughness, as well as smoothness for bearing use, is provided by molding a sleeve to be press-fitted or heat-shrunk onto a metal shaft.

Solution coating with phenolic solvents is possible above 170°F. Parachlorophenol or dimethyl formamide may be used, although solids content of solvents up to 300°F is less than 5 per cent. Dispersion coating with similar solvents or cyclohexanol as fluxing agent is covered in United States Patent 2,791,000.

4. BEARINGS

Acetal resin deserves consideration for bearings because:

(1) when completely lubricated, bearings of acetal perform similarly to metal bearings;

(2) they can be used with little or no lubrication;

(3) they have very low coefficients of friction (down to 0.1 when unlubricated and 0.05 when lubricated);

(4) they show no slip-stick behavior because there is no noticeable difference between the dynamic and static coefficients of friction against steel.

The major reasons for choosing plastics for bearings are light weight and ability to be molded into intricate designs. Thus, part and assembly costs may be reduced by combining in one molding a shaft, driving gear, cam, and bearings. Acetal has low creep, that is, a low deformation under load even at high humidities and temperatures. While its heat deformation temperature at 66 psi (ASTM D 648) is 338°F, acetal should not be used as a bearing in continuous service above 180°F, nor intermittently above 250°F. These temperatures, however, are much higher than the generally accepted principle that a bearing should not run hotter than handwarm. The major reason for limiting service temperature is the thermal expansion of the material, which reduces clearances and in turn rapidly accelerates further heating, even to melting of the bearing surface.

Acetal is only slightly affected by environment. It is practically inert to most solvents. Although it is not suitable for use in strong acids or bases, the corrosion resistance of acetal approaches that of plated brass, high-carbon steels and even many stainless steels. Changes in humidity produce almost no dimensional changes, and the material functions at high service temperatures with little loss of modulus. Its high strength and resilience permit press-fits and snap-fits. The resiliency tends to damp vibration and thus will tolerate larger clearances in bearing assemblies.

The performance limits suggested in this chapter are based on many tests in laboratory and field installations, which have reasonably established the operational range for bearings of acetal.

Figure 4.1 plots actual applications versus pressure and velocity. Regardless of the material, there is no accurate way of calculating the performance of the bearing, even if all the design factors are known. However, an approximation can be reached which will indicate whether a specific bearing is able to do a required job. By calculating the bearing loads and speeds, to arrive at a pressure and velocity factor (called the *PV* value), the engineer will be able to assess the general utility of a bearing or at least to obtain the substantiation needed to justify further tests which would simulate operating conditions. This *PV* factor calculation is normally employed in the design of many metal bearings.

The *PV* value is the product of pressure (the load in psi of the projected bearing area) and the velocity (surface speed in feet per minute). For sleeve bearings, the projected area is that of a plane running through the bearing along its axis, of the same length and of a width equal to the diameter of the bearing. Thus for a bearing .70 inch in diameter and .50 inch long, the projected area is 0.35 square inch. If the revolutions per minute, the total load, the bearing length, and the shaft diameter are known, the *PV* value for any given

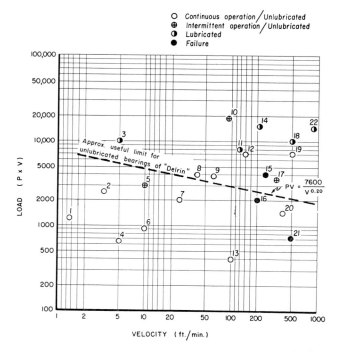

Figure 4.1. Load and speed conditions of practical applications.

1. Door hinges
2. Whiproll bearings
3. Pump bearing—wick lubricated
4. Caster bearing
5. Lift truck bearing
6. Cart wheel bearing
7. Saddle bearing
8. Supermarket cart wheel bearing
9. Split sleeve bearing—lab test
10. Closet door roller
11. Ring bearing
12. Split sleeve bearing—lab test
13. Shaver connecting rod bearing

bearing can be calculated. From this value the physical dimensions of the bearing needed for a specific application can be determined. Table 4.1 provides a table to convert diameters and revolutions per minute to the velocity factor in the *PV* table.

Short of changing speed conditions, the only design variable of a sliding friction bearing which has any effect on the *PV* value is its length. Thus if the bearing length is fixed at about the generally recommended 1:1 ratio of length to diameter, only a reduction of speed or load can bring the bearing into a useful operating range. Conversely, if speed and load are fixed, only a change in length (which reduces the unit load by increasing the projected area) can bring the design within the allowable *PV* limit. This is true, because a change in shaft diameter to increase the projected area also increases the running speed in feet per minute by about the same ratio.

On a cost basis acetal competes with metals commonly used as bearing materials. At a cubic inch cost of less than 4 cents, the lightness of acetal makes it competitive with copper alloys and steels, which range from 6 to 15 cents per cubic inch. Bearings injection-molded of acetal even in quantities of a few hundred rather than thousands can be more economical than fabrication by methods usually employed with metals.

---

14. 1 inch journal bearing
15. Automobile D-C generator bearing (operating temperature too high, rapid wear)
16. Electric fan bearing (wear and spot melting due to insufficient clearance)
17. Spinnerette bearing
18. Engine connecting rod bearing
19. Split sleeve bearing—lab test
20. Yarn guide
21. Elevator gibs (wear due to unequal loads)
22. Conveyor wheel bushing

TABLE 4.1. CONVERSION DATA FOR CALCULATIONS OF RPM TO FPM.

$$FPM = RPM \times \frac{\pi d}{12}$$

where d is the diameter of the shaft (or housing, whichever is the running surface) in inches.

$$\frac{\pi}{12} = 0.262 \qquad FPM = RPM \times d \times 0.262$$

The values of $\frac{\pi d}{12}$ for some basic bearing shaft diameters are:

Diameter d (in.)	$\frac{\pi d}{12}$	Diameter d (in.)	$\frac{\pi d}{12}$
1/16	0.02	1	0.26
1/8	0.03	2	0.52
3/16	0.05	3	0.78
1/4	0.07	4	1.05
5/16	0.08	5	1.31
3/8	0.10	6	1.57
7/16	0.11	7	1.83
1/2	0.13	8	2.09
9/16	0.15	9	2.36
5/8	0.16	10	2.62
11/16	0.18	11	2.88
3/4	0.20	12	3.14
13/16	0.21	13	3.40
7/8	0.23	14	3.66
15/16	0.25	15	3.93

Intermediate values can be obtained by adding the value of $\frac{\pi d}{12}$ for full inches to that of fractions. Thus, $\frac{\pi d}{12}$ for a shaft 1 1/16 inches $= 0.26 + 0.02 = 0.28$.

Since acetal can be machined as easily as free-cutting brass, making prototypes from bar stock is not difficult, and permits the designer to run prototype tests. In general, bearing calculations should only be used to determine basic feasibility of a design and to indicate if it is worthwhile to run confirming tests.

FACTORS AFFECTING BEARING DESIGN

Clearance

Nothing is quite so basic to the design of a plastic bearing as proper running clearance on the shaft or the housing. Clearance is defined as the difference between the diameter of the shaft and the diameter of the bearing. Thus "clearance" as understood in bearing design is twice the radial space between the bearing and the shaft. Clearances for plastics are generally much larger than for metal bearings. However, such clearances are necessary and beneficial in many ways.

For thermoplastics such as acetal, generous clearances help to improve service life, particularly of unlubricated bearings. Clearances of as much as .015 inch per inch of shaft diameter are not uncommon. The resilience and vibration absorption of acetal aid in overcoming possible disadvantages in large clearances. Basic clearance for a continuously lubricated bearing can be as little as .002 inch per inch of shaft diameter for bearing diameters around 1 inch, and .004 inch per inch for shafts around 3 inch diameter. The basic clearance may go up to .008 inch per inch for larger bearings. The basic clearance for a completely unlubricated bearing should not be less than .005 inch per inch of shaft diameter.

As in the case of casting tolerances with metals, molding tolerances must be allowed for when dealing with plastics. Dimensional tolerances normally achieved with acetal are: for commercial molding, .003 inch per inch for the first inch or fraction, and .002 inch per inch for subsequent inches; for precision molding, usually at some higher cost for mold and molding, the tolerance may be .002 inch per inch for the first inch and .001 inch per inch for subsequent inches.

Several design and service factors influence the clearance

requirements and each factor should be considered before the
final design. These factors explained in detail below are:

(1) Lubrication
(2) Temperature
(3) Press- or snap-fits
(4) Types of service and motion
(5) Friction and wear

Lubrication. Lubrication can make considerable difference in required clearances. Thus while acetal can be run
without any lubrication, this should be done only when abso-
lutely necessary. Varying degrees of lubrication affect performance and clearances, as indicated in Table 4.2 and 4.4.

TABLE 4.2. CLEARANCE SUGGESTED FOR VARIOUS SHAFT DIAMETERS
FOR EXPECTED TEMPERATURE RANGES.*

Shaft Diameter	Room Temperature to +140°F	Room Temperature to +250°F	−50° to +250°F
Unlubricated Bearings			
¼″	0.003″	0.004″	0.006″
½″	0.004″	0.008″	0.010″
¾″	0.006″	0.012″	0.015″
1″	0.008″	0.015″	0.020″
1¼″	0.010″	0.018″	0.025″
1½″	0.012″	0.021″	0.030″
Lubricated Bearings			
Per inch of shaft diameter	0.003–0.005″	0.007–0.010″	0.015–0.020″

"Clearance" here is the difference between shaft and bearing
diameter. It is twice the annular space at bearing surface.

For intermediate shaft diameters and different temperature ranges,
it is suggested that the actual clearance requirements be calculated
from thermal expansion data added to a basic clearance of 0.005 inch
per inch of shaft diameter.

* Fabrication tolerances must also be considered.

Continuous lubrication will allow closer tolerance limits and give better performance in terms of greater load or speed. Occasional lubrication will give higher than unlubricated performance, but clearances must be the same as for no lubrication at all. Lubrication, even if applied only at installation, will give improvements over performance limits of completely unlubricated bearings. Increasing lubrication reduces the need for larger clearances and raises the performance limits.

Temperature. Temperature enters into the design of clearances for two reasons: (1) all plastics have a coefficient of thermal expansion roughly tenfold that of metals; and (2) plastics dissipate heat more slowly than do metals. Temperature rise can be caused by operation or by environment, such as under the hood of an automobile. One of the first steps should be to determine the temperature range over which the bearing must operate, using the upper and lower expected environmental temperatures at maximum RPM.

Without thermocouples it is difficult to measure actual equilibrium running temperature. However, if the bearing is at all within the suggested *PV* value limits, equilibrium running temperature should not be critical. Table 4.2 gives approximate clearance suggested for different temperature ranges. For exact calculations the data of Table 4.6 should be used.

Thermal expansion must be considered for both lubricated and unlubricated bearings. Some designs, such as slotted sleeves, may offer a partial solution but, basically, thermal expansion must be included until tests show that reduction in clearances can be employed because of cooling, or good heat dissipation through the shaft and housing.

Be realistic about the temperature range selected. Naturally the widest range possible should be covered, but a practical approach may bring a bearing from failure to success. Food mixer bearings need not be designed for operation at $-40°F$, for example, nor should a textile bearing be designed for operation at $250°F$ when it is never subjected to more than $110°F$.

Table 4.2 shows clearance values calculated from the thermal expansion data in Table 4.6, and based on thermal expansion over the temperature ranges here shown. The clearance values for various shaft diameters are those which should be used for room temperature installation. Their use will provide a minimum clearance of .005 inch per inch of shaft diameter through the expected temperature range.

Press- and Snap-fits. The resilience and excellent compressive strength of acetal allow press-fits (a fit under continuous load) and snap-fits (snapping over an interference, but not under continuous load). Generally, no additional clearance need be allowed for snap-fits unless the interference over which the bearing is snapped exceeds the elastic recovery. When press-fitting a bearing of acetal, allow additional clearance equal to the interference. In a press-fit the interference will translate itself almost completely into a close-in on the internal diameter or an expansion of the outside diameter, whichever is the running surface. The calculated running clearance will not be affected if the interference has been included in the design.

Types of Service and Motion. The clearances discussed so far pertain to continuously running journal bearings. Recommended basic clearances usually suffice in cases where a sharp rise in operating temperature will not occur, such as intermittent operation, frequent start and stop motion, reciprocal motion, linear or helical sliding motion, occasional peak loading, or air-, water- or oil-cooled operation. Figure 4.1 shows that bearings for these types of service or motion usually performed above the *PV* value limit for unlubricated bearings. The multitude of possible combinations precludes testing all of them. However, available data indicate that under some of these service or motion conditions, minimum *PV* values can be as much as doubled.

Friction and Wear. Tests of bearings have indicated a tendency toward a linear relationship between the rate of wear and coefficient of friction. In general the tighter the clearance, the higher the coefficient of friction and the higher the wear rate. High friction can build up heat fast enough to cause partial or complete melting. Up to 250°F and about 2500 psi load, neither heat nor load appears to affect the friction. However, a tight clearance may increase the angle of contact of the bearing with the shaft, in which case coefficients of friction will be higher.

Loads and Speeds

It has thus far been possible to describe all laboratory and field performance by converting data to the standard *PV* factor. The *PV* values discussed here are those for maximum useful operation with no lubrication. This means that a bearing had to complete five million cycles of continuous running without significant wear, with coefficient of friction not higher than 0.35, and with all traces of lubricant on shaft and bearing removed with a solvent. This is the area of operation where metals do not ordinarily work. Numerous runs with lubricated bearings showed coefficient of friction consistently between 0.05 and 0.15, no excessive heating, and practically no wear at speeds up to 2,000 RPM.

The formula for such unlubricated bearing performance with a minimum clearance of 0.005 inch per inch of shaft diameter is

$$PV = \frac{7600}{V^{0.20}}$$

Figure 4.2 shows this curve as a dotted line. For a quick survey this formula approximates the useful limit of $PV = 1600$ and Figure 4.2 shows this relationship as the solid line.

Table 4.3 shows the limiting PV values for various speeds of unlubricated bearings. Table 4.4 shows the range of PV values for various types of lubrication.

From the curve of the formula $PV = \dfrac{7600}{V^{0.20}}$ it can be seen that speed is the controlling factor, rather than load. V cannot be adjusted significantly by changing the diameter of the bearing, being a function of the circumference. Any adjust-

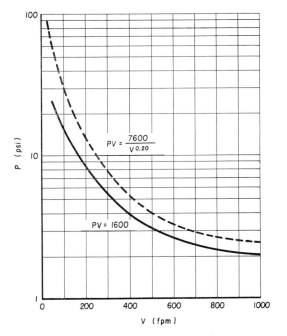

Figure 4.2. Useful PV range, unlubricated bearings of "Delrin."

TABLE 4.3. APPROXIMATE PERFORMANCE VALUES UNLUBRICATED, STEEL SHAFT, ACETAL JOURNAL.

Speed (FPM)	Limiting *PV*
0-100	3000
100-200	2600
200-400	2200
400-600	2100
600-1000	1900

ment toward achieving a lower *PV* value must come from a change in the projected bearing area which lowers the unit load. There is some latitude for increasing the length of the bearing; but caution should be exercised to avoid increasing the diameter, as this increases the speed at the surface of the bearing. The ratio of length to diameter of 1:1 has been found most suitable with acetal, and a departure too far from this may cause spot wear or even spot melting.

One word of caution is advisable: When using these empirical *PV* formulas, less dependence should be placed upon them when approaching the extremes of either all load and almost no speed, or all speed and almost no load. The *PV* values should be used for initial evaluations only, to be

TABLE 4.4. DEPENDENCE OF *PV* ON TYPE OF LUBRICATION.

(Continuous operation, no wear-in period)

Continuous	Mean *PV* Value at Various Speeds
Completely unlubricated	1600-2000
Lubricated at installation	3000-5000
Repeated lubrication	5000-10,000
Continuous lubrication	10,000-15,000+

followed by testing of prototypes, under conditions simulating actual use as nearly as possible.

It should also be remembered that differences in service conditions and lubrication and types of motion can raise the *PV* limits. For short periods the listed *PV* values may be exceeded by as much as 25 per cent. A wear-in period can also add to performance, especially if initial lubrication can be tolerated.

Lubrication

Throughout this chapter, reference is made to data on the various conditions of lubrication. To avoid misconception, these terms are explained, and may be different from those commonly used with metal bearings.

(1) No lubrication or completely unlubricated refers to a condition in which both the bearing and the shaft were wiped dry with a solvent. After solvent cleaning the shaft and bearing were handled with gloves to avoid contamination with skin oils. No lubricant whatever was added after installation or during the entire test period.

(2) Initial lubrication or lubricated at installation refers to 3 to 5 drops of oil added when the bearing was assembled, but none thereafter.

(3) Repeated lubrication goes beyond the initial lubrication in that a few drops of oil were added infrequently during operation, simulating a condition of occasional maintenance.

(4) Continuous lubrication refers to a constant supply of lubricant. Under this condition wear is lowest and friction least. This condition can approach what bearing theory calls boundary, hydrodynamic, or force lubrication. Under the latter, the *PV* values are so high they become meaningless.

Oils and Greases. Acetal is resistant to most commonly used oils, greases, or hydrocarbon compounds such as kerosene and high octane fuels. The presence of these lubricants at elevated temperatures has little effect on acetal nor does acetal affect them. A possible exception is prolonged service in hot recirculating motor oils which might result in an accumulation of acidic contaminants in the oil which could be detrimental to acetal.

Water up to a *PV* value of 2,000 to 3,000 can be a very effective lubricant. This is probably because water acts as a dissipator of heat. Bearings which are occasionally cleaned with water, steam, or solvents will not be affected unless they were designed for lubricated operation and the cleaning has removed the lubricant. In such cases relubrication is required. Underwater operation of a bearing of acetal is not detrimental. However, for long periods of submersion see Figures 2.6 and 2.7 about dimensional considerations in designing such bearings.

Trace lubrication by annealing is possible in that if a bearing is molded or machined and then annealed in hot oil a small amount of oil can be incorporated. Penetration up to a depth of about .010 inch has been achieved. This process at times reduces wear and allows a slightly higher *PV* value. Depending upon whether or not the bearings are wiped dry after annealing, the amount of lubrication varies from a trace to the initial lubrication. The process of annealing has other beneficial effects and is described in Chapter 3.

Dry Lubricants. Because of the difficulty of administering such lubricants, quantitative definition of the improvements which they might contribute has not been established.

Other Lubricants. Most tests have been conducted with commonly used hydrocarbon oils and greases because they are usually effective. Some special lubricants which have been tested and found more effective than petroleum fluids in reducing wear and increasing the allowable *PV* values are:

"Primol D" of Esso Standard Oil Company, Silicone Oil 710 of Dow Corning Company, and "Vydax A" fluorocarbon dispersion of E. I. du Pont de Nemours & Company.

Anti-friction Fillers. Various materials, such as graphite, molybdenum disulfide, aluminum stearate and other stearates, tetrafluoroethylene resin and fibers and petroleum hydrocarbons, have been used singly and in combination as fillers for plastics to reduce friction and improve the bearing characteristics. High-spot tests show that these materials seldom give more than a marginal improvement in the bearing performance of "Delrin," as they are generally incompatible.

Wear and Wear-in

In a few cases, under excessive loads and speeds or with insufficient clearances, failure of a bearing will occur as a result of rapid heat build-up beyond the melting point of acetal, which is 348°F. The majority of unsuccessful bearing applications show that excessive loads or speeds increase wear in apparent linear proportion to the increase in load or speed. If wear occurs below suggested loads or speeds, it is almost always due to insufficient clearance, lack of lubrication, or the presence of dust, rust, or sand.

Higher-than-expected wear can also be due to the deficiencies of mating surface against which bearing of acetal is running. In general, acetal behaves like other bearing materials in that it performs better against dissimilar materials than against itself. The following illustrations of bearing and shaft material refer to a no-lubrication condition.

Acetal to Steel. Most frictional data from field and laboratory tests are from this combination, which has shown the lowest coefficients of friction and lowest wear rates.

Acetal to Aluminum. Here the coefficients of friction tend to be higher than against steel. Corrosion of the aluminum, such as in salt-water service, tends to increase the wear of acetal severely. There are also indications that aluminum has a tendency to spall or flake off, introducing the new particles in the bearing interface area, rapidly increasing the wear.

Acetal to Acetal. While this bearing combination is not the most desirable, it cannot be avoided in some applications. It should be remembered that two equally low heat conductors are mated; hence heat build-up during operation will be more rapid than when run against metals. Under very light loads, this combination performs well. With increasing loads and speeds, both components should be annealed or lubricated.

Acetal to Nylon Resin. The same arguments as for acetal-to-acetal generally apply. It has been found, however, that the combination of acetal to nylon is noticeably better than a combination of acetal to acetal. The frictional similarity and chemical dissimilarity of these two materials make this combination the one most worth trying where a bearing of acetal must run against another high-strength plastic.

Acetal to Other Plastics. The same caution should be noted here as in acetal-to-acetal, in that the problem is the mating of poor heat conductors. Lubrication is suggested if the mating plastic is resistant to the lubricant. It has been established that acetal usually outwears laminated thermosetting resins 4 to 6 times, and even more when run in the presence of moisture. Applications where acetal must run against a thermoplastic or thermosetting resin should be tested carefully. Variations in thermal expansion, hardness, or abrasion resistance of the mating shaft can cause unexpected reductions in clearances and the wear rates may be higher.

Surface Finish

Primarily, it is more the condition of the surface of the mating metal part than the metal itself which produces wear.

Metal shafts need not be hardened. However, commercial polishing is a definite aid in reducing wear. Shaft finishes of 8 to 12 RMS have given the lowest wear, with wear rates increasing as shaft roughness increases. The bearing surface of acetal is much less critical. Molded or machined surfaces of 25 to 45 RMS may be used. Rougher surfaces initially produce a higher wear, but seem to level off after a wear-in period. The hardness of acetal, as in metals, does not change significantly between $-70°F$ and $300°F$, so allowance need not be made for a change in indentation hardness.

A wear-in or break-in period before applying maximum service loads and speeds is recommended. A wear-in period of as little as 15 minutes has been known to double the allowable loads. When testing under several conditions, the use of separate bearings for each run is recommended. This is to avoid trials with bearings which have been worn in, which might not be typical of all field conditions. Since a gradual increase of load and speed will raise the allowable *PV* limit, failure in the field might occur if such a gradual wear-in period were not used.

Friction

In a bearing application so many factors are inter-related that it is difficult to distinguish between individual causes and results. Frictional properties of acetal are influenced by load, speed and lubrication. The frictional properties themselves influence wear rate, ambient running temperature, and the general performance such as drag and power loss.

Figure 4.3 and Table 4.5 show the mean values for coefficients of friction. They were determined on bearing testers with a graphical record of temperature, coefficient of friction, load and speed. When unlubricated, coefficients of friction beyond a *PV* value of 2,000 rise to a point of about 0.35,

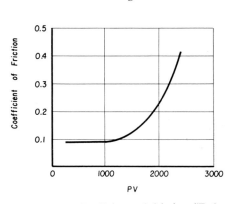

Figure 4.3. Coefficient of friction "Del-rin" to steel, annealed, no lubrication.

TABLE 4.5. RANGE IN COEFFICIENT OF FRICTION.
Acetal-on-Steel/Inclined Plane Method

Condition	Coefficient of Friction	
	Static	Dynamic
Oil lubricated		
(Viscosity 58 SSU/100°F)		
Maximum	0.1	0.1
Minimum	0.05	0.05
Water lubricated		
Maximum	0.2	0.2
Minimum	0.1	0.1
No lubricant		
Maximum	0.3	0.3
Minimum	0.1	0.1

These values were established over a load range of from 0.5-2500 psi.

These values were established over a speed range of from 8-367 fpm.

These values were established over a temperature range of from 73-250°F.

which induces faster wear rate. An increase in lubrication will decrease coefficient of friction to 0.05 until boundary lubrication theory takes over and no actual bearing-to-shaft contact remains. Since there is no difference between the dynamic and static coefficients of friction for acetal on steel, there is no slip-stick; that is, starting and running friction are the same. Similarly with *PV* values, which tend to be less predictable under conditions approaching the all-speed or the all-load end of the *PV* curve; the coefficients of friction may be higher or lower at these extreme conditions. Temperatures up to about 250°F do not seem to affect coefficients of friction. As determined by the inclined plane method, coefficients of friction are not increased by loads up to 2,500 psi.

The reason that reduced clearances increase friction, and thus heat and wear, seems to be that, due to the resilience of acetal, a smaller clearance will increase contact area of the shaft upon the bearing. The effect of reduced clearance or increased angular contact is most evident in sleeve bearings, where the operating heat has caused the ends to bow in slightly to produce barrel cross-section. Reduced clearance can also be caused by stress relief of the molded bearing during an annealing operation. If localized wear or seizing occurs after the bearing has once run successfully, stressed conditions of the molded part may be the cause. They can be particularly evident in sample parts molded from trial cavities for initial tests. Test samples should be inspected for roundness and preferably should be annealed and wiped clean.

Factors Affecting Dimensional Stability

Around room temperature the coefficient of linear expansion of acetal is 4.5×10^{-5} per °F. Table 4.6 shows change of expansion coefficient with temperature. Thermal conductivity of acetal is 1.6 Btu per hour per square foot per degree

TABLE 4.6. EFFECT OF TEMPERATURE ON DIMENSIONS OF ACETAL.

(ASTM D 696)

Temperature Range (°F)	Coefficient of Linear Thermal Expansion (in./in./°F)	°F to Produce 1 mil/in. Change in Dimension
85	4.5×10^{-5}	22
85–140	5.5×10^{-5}	18
140–220	6.0×10^{-5}	17

Fahrenheit per inch. The first value is nearly ten times that common with metals, while the latter value is much lower than in metals.

The greater the temperature range over which a bearing of acetal must work, the greater the expansion involved. The bearing should have a minimum clearance of 0.005 inch per inch at the lowest temperature at which operation is expected. Thermal expansion will work both over diameter and over length. The latter should not be of consequence if the bearing is unrestricted at least at one end. If the bearing is restricted at both ends and localized wear or spot melting appears on test, it may be due to an end-compressive effect. Either longitudinal or diametric clearance should be enlarged. The thinner the plastic bearing, the better the heat transfer through the housing and shaft. In some cases temperature effects can be overcome by easily molded special bearing designs incorporating spiral or straight oil grooves, expansion slots, or perforated walls, without raising clearances to unacceptable values.

Annealing

Since a molded bearing during the fabrication process goes from a melt to a solid, some residual stresses may be frozen in. In time the stresses may relieve themselves. In a bearing this is usually evidenced by reduction in clearance and subsequent seizing. Temperature can hasten this strain relief. That is why bearings that run hot will frequently run successfully once, but will seize before the second start-up. Whatever stresses are frozen into the molded part can be relieved by heat. This annealing is generally done in an oil medium which also lubricates the bearing. The annealing temperature should be higher than the expected service or ambient running temperature.

Annealing of acetal should be carried out in the absence of air, preferably by immersion in a suitable annealing oil. The oil should be stable at the annealing temperature, should not attack acetal or give off noxious vapors. Refined medicinal mineral oil or lubricating oil has been satisfactory.

The recommended annealing temperature is $320°F \pm 3°$. Oil temperature should not exceed $323°F$, as that may cause deterioration of the physical properties of the part or cause some warpage. Figure 4.4 shows the necessary annealing time for sections up to 1 inch thick. The average thickness of the part may be used to determine proper annealing time.

Annealed pieces should be removed from the bath and cooled in air to room temperature, preferably in a draft-free container. Accelerated cooling must be avoided, as it might introduce new thermal stress into the skin of the hot plastic.

Moisture

Acetal is one of the thermoplastics least affected by moisture. However, possible dimensional change due to service in water should be included in the design. Figure 2.7 provides a method for approximating dimensional changes due to temperature and moisture. Figure 2.5 indicates the time taken for these changes to occur. Usually only prolonged

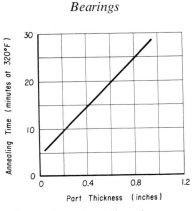

Figure 4.4. Annealing time *vs.*
thickness.

service at immersion or similar conditions requires consideration of the change in dimensions with moisture.

Creep

The strain recovery and creep resistance of acetal are very
good, particularly under conditions of high temperature and
humidity. For all practical bearing applications, the loads
allowable for good operation of acetal are below the stress
level causing deformation over time (creep). Therefore it
is seldom that design allowances need be made for creep.
There are, however, some bearing applications where creep
must be considered as a design checkpoint. Such are bearings
to support a load for an extended period of time under static
conditions. However many bearing applications in this category (such as rollers from which hang sliding doors) have
exhibited only insignificant amounts of creep.

Holding a Bearing in Place

Several methods can be employed to hold a bearing or
bushing in its assigned place. The least desirable method

from the standpoint of acetal would be to constrict the ends of the bearing. Prevention of thermal expansion in the axial direction may increase the radial expansion and dangerously reduce the necessary shaft clearance.

A key arrangement is frequently used and is attractive because the key can be molded into the acetal bearing at the time of manufacture.

A snap-fit is practical where a bearing can be forced over an interference and then held in place without being under continuous load, such as would be from a press-fit. Press-fits onto a shaft or into a housing are feasible. However, the amount of interference must be added to design clearance, as the resilience of acetal transfers interference, closing the inside diameter of the bearing when press-fitted into housing, or expanding outer diameter when pressed onto shaft. Acetal can be press-fit onto a shaft up to 0.050 inch per interference, depending somewhat upon the shaft-to-hub outside diameter ratio. Standard interference calculations apply and are indicated in Figure 4.5.

Flanges can be used to hold the bearing in place and so can set screws. While a pilot hole is needed to insert the set screw the hole usually does not need to be tapped.

Check Points for Design of Bearings of Acetal

Bearing should in general be designed to be at or below the suggested *PV* limits for the particular type of lubrication anticipated.

Clearances should contain allowances for thermal expansion over the operating temperature range, for press-fit effects, for expansion due to moisture and for fabrication tolerances.

Type of service and motion should be considered particularly where it is intermittent or reciprocal or where there may be occasional peak loading.

A designer's check list is given in Table 4.7 which tabulates possible difficulties and remedies. The remedial actions are listed in their increasing order of complexity.

Remedies:

A. Friction properties
    Use wear-in period
    Anneal
    Lubricate initially, intermittently, or continuously
B. Minor design changes
    Increase clearance
    Remove end restrictions
    Increase length
    Decrease speed
    Decrease load

C. Assembly changes
    Check alignment
    Check roundness
    Check straightness
    Use smoother shaft or bearing
    Reduce shock loading
D. Major design changes
    Use thinner wall
    Use split or slotted bearing
    Use cooling

Exact prediction of bearing performance is prevented by minor differences in load, speed, alignment, lubrication and environment. This is true even with bearing materials on which years of experience have developed intuitive judgment as to practical sizes. Accordingly, with plastic bearings, prototypes should be made unless the proposed use is obviously not critical. To determine whether prototyping is unnecessary because of light duty, advisable because of promise, or unwarranted because of severity of conditions—the first step should be estimation of PV factor. Next, the PV factor should be compared with Figure 4.1 and discussion of the following diverse uses.

Additional bearings are discussed in Chapters 8 and 9. Simple bushings of acetal are used where lubrication is not wanted, or may be provided by water. Such a use is in split bushings for clothes washer wringers; or the hand can opener of Figure 4.6, which shows grooves molded into bearing for staking together the operating key and gear which rotates the can.

TABLE 4.7. TROUBLE-SHOOTING GUIDE, WITH REMEDIES LISTED IN ORDER OF INCREASING COMPLEXITY.

Problem	Possible Cause	Possible Remedy			
General wear	Insufficient clearance	A	B	C	D
	Excessive load or speed	A	B	C	D
	Bearing is barrel shaped	A	B	C	
	Misalignment			C	
	Trapped wear particles	A	B	C	D
	Impact or shock loading	A		C	
Localized wear	Bearing is barrel shaped	A	B	C	
Melting	Excessive speed	A	B		D
	Excessive load	A	B		D
Fracture	Impact or shock loading			C	
	Misalignment			C	
High friction	Insufficient clearance	A	B		D
	Trapped wear particles	A	B	C	D
	End restriction		B		D
	Excessive speed	A	B		D
	Excessive load	A	B		D
	Rough surface contacting			C	
Seizure during or	Insufficient clearance	A	B		D
after operation	Excessive speed	A	B		D
	Excessive load	A	B		D
	Excessive service temperature				D

CLOTHES DRYER DRUM BEARING

The unusual combination of acetal on porcelain is used as bearing in clothes dryer shown in Figure 4.7. The usual design has been to support the drum entirely from the bearing tube at rear, which required massive pylon to support a 45 pound load at 47 revolutions per minute. The new design fastens a one-piece molded ring of acetal inside the open end of the drum. This ring slides on porcelain shoes near top of cabinet. Minimal lubrication is provided by felt wick. Needed are good frictional properties, some resilience, and

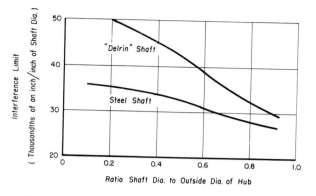

Figure 4.5. Theoretical interference limits for press fitting "Delrin." Based on yield point and elastic modulus at room temperature.

dimensional stability at 200°F with humid and dry air. Quiet performance is achieved and savings result from use of a less massive pylon at rear, and elimination of need to custom-locate each drum on the single mount in order to get proper spacing at front. The molded ring is held to circumference of 43.88 to 44.00 inch, and 0.5 inch out-of-round, after annealing an hour at 250°F in paraffin oil.

This use is a good example of calculations to determine feasibility before constructing prototype. To calculate the *PV* factor, the following information was used:

Drum circumference: 44 inches
Load: drum 25 pounds plus 20 pounds wet clothes; to be supported equally between shaft and ring, giving load on acetal of 22.5 pounds.
Speed: 47 rpm

To reduce swing of drum, it was proposed to use two shoes 3 x 0.62 inches, each 45° from top center of drum. Each

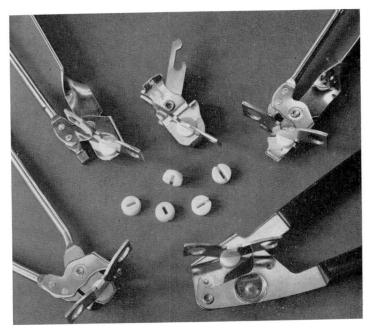

Figure 4.6. Hand can opener.

shoe supports half of front load, or one-quarter of total load 45 pounds, or 11.3 pounds.

$$P = \frac{\text{radial load}}{\text{shoe area}} = \frac{\text{vertical load}}{\cos 45° \times 1.86} = \frac{11.3 \times \sqrt{2}}{1.86} = 8.6 \text{ psi}$$

$$V = \frac{44}{12} \times 47 = 172 \text{ feet per minute}$$

$$PV = 8.6 \times 172 = 1480$$

From Figures 4.1, 4.2, and Table 4.4, it is seen that a PV of 1480 with initial lubrication makes the proposed use and geometry quite promising; commercial production has amply fulfilled this expectation.

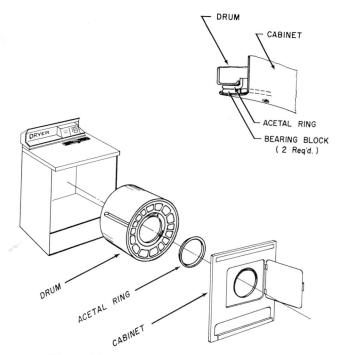

Figure 4.7. Clothes dryer drum bearing ring.

ROLLER CONVEYOR SHAFT BEARINGS

Roller conveyors are used for much gravity handling of packages. Rollers have usually been made from steel tube with ball or roller bearings inserted at ends, a succession of these rollers then being mounted on steel frames. Acetal sleeve bearings are used in roller conveyors to provide quieter operation and more economical units. Figure 4.8 shows the assembly with molded acetal ring (in white) and the more complex ball-bearing race which it replaced. Acetal pro-

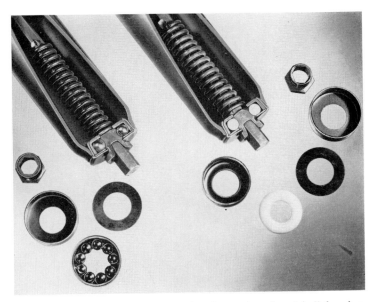

Figure 4.8. Roller conveyor ring bearing and replaced ball bearing.

vides dimensional stability under range of humidities and temperatures, and resistance to developing flat spots under prolonged static loads.

Strips of acetal are used as guide rails for metal-link conveyors. They have good performance under abrasive conditions; and are used in commercial dishwashers where lubricants are objectionable, or would be removed by detergent.

Good bearing properties are needed in flat-top-link conveyor belts, used in many packaging or bottle-washing lines. In some cases, an acetal plate may be fastened to a metal link, by heading over a stud molded into bottom of acetal plate. In others, the plate is molded with integral lugs, and

Figure 4.9. Flat-top conveyor links.

chain is made simply by inserting steel pin through lugs of adjacent links. Acetal links are quiet and do not chip glass containers. They operate with little or no lubricant, hence may be used in detergent baths. They are enough lighter in weight than metal chains to reduce power needs to less than

Figure 4.10. Molded chain and sprocket.

half. In a few instances, acetal has displaced nylon links because of its lesser stretch under load, important as some of
the chains are over a hundred feet long. Figure 4.9 shows
link-tops with integral lugs and also tops fastened by studs
headed into all-metal chains.

SPROCKETS AND LINK CHAINS

Sprocket chains must be made from material of good bearing properties, and acetal combines these with toughness and stiffness. Figure 4.10 shows molded acetal links which are snapped together to make chain for mechanisms requiring low inertia and backlash, and absence of electrical contact between units. Chain is assembled by snap-fitting molded links. Master links are not needed and the chain length can be changed easily by increments of a single link. One size weighs but an ounce for 15 feet, is tested for running loads of 2 pounds and momentary loads up to 7 pounds.

5. GEARS

Plastics are being increasingly used for gears and cams, both for economy and for performance. Economy comes from the ease with which gears may be injection-molded, rarely needing a finishing operation. Significant savings are possible when in one molding there is combined one or more gears with shaft, bearings or cam. Size and part numbers can also be molded into the piece.

Performance has been a major factor in the choice of molded plastics versus metals for gears only since the advent of plastics with good stiffness, dimensional stability and fatigue properties. As indicated in the introductory chapter, choice of plastic should be made after comparison of many properties. When stresses or environment may be severe, a prototype should be machined for test under conditions of actual use.

Plastics chosen for gears are usually those with low coefficient of friction—important when little or no lubricant is to be used. Acetal and nylon resins work well with water as lubricant, and have been preferred to metal because they can be lubricated by food liquids, detergents, or salt and mild acid or alkali, which are corrosive to metals. At low stresses in these environments or in some dusty conditions, plastic gears outwear those made from commonly used metals.

For smooth and quiet operation, dimensional tolerances for plastic gears are less critical than for metal gears. The inherent resilience of plastics enables them to conform to variations in concentricity, pitch and profile; damps vibration

110

or transmission of shock loading; and permits spreading load over more than one tooth.

Most plastic gears are spur gears, which have the shape easiest to mold. Worm, bevel, helical and rack and pinion sets have been molded or machined from solid stock. There seems to be no basic limitation as to type of gear which will affect choice of the plastic material.

Plastics Materials for Gears

For gear use, plastics usually narow to four families: acetal, carbonate, nylon, and certain blends of acrylonitrile-butadiene-styrene, called ABS resins. Modifications are possible within each family; hence strict relative ratings are not valid for all uses. Table 5.1 does provide ratings for representative compositions, and suggests points to be considered in evaluations. It also points out that change of environment or stress may greatly alter choice of material.

TABLE 5.1. APPROXIMATE RATING OF VALUE IN GEAR USAGE

1 = Best   4 = Poorest   X = Utility doubtful

	Acetal	Carbonate	Nylon	ABS
Impact—single	4	2	3	1
Impact—fatigue	2	3	1	4
Flexure fatigue	1	3	2	4
Dimensional stability				
in water	3	2	4	1
in lube oil	1	4X	2	3X
Chemical resistance				
acid	2X	3X	4X	1
aikali	2	4X	3	1
solvent	1	4	2	3
Stiffness				
room temperature	2	3	4	1
at 200°F	1	2	3	4
Abrasion resistance	2	3	1	4

The nylon used for gears is usually type 66 (hexamethylene adipamide) because of its superior stiffness and resistance to fatigue and wear. The following examples will indicate factors which may influence decision between acetal and nylon resins. In a lawn mower pinion, nylon was preferred because of impact loading. In clocks and cameras, acetal resin has displaced some nylon uses because acetal moldings have better dimensional stability under varying humidity. In vending machines, acetal was preferred because of low creep under stalled loading.

Major reasons for choice of acetal or nylon for gears are often thought to be their high resistance to abrasion and their low coefficient of friction. In practice, resistance to fatigue or deformation by stall loads is frequently the reason for choosing acetal above all other plastics. Where load is eccentric, or gear and shaft are not exactly concentric, the loading is cyclical, and fatigue endurance may become decisive.

Lubrication plays an important role. When gears are continuously lubricated, load-carrying capacity is determined by bending fatigue strength for both acetal and nylon; each has fatigue endurance beyond other commercial thermoplastics. Bending fatigue still determines the capacity of nylon; wear is the limiting factor for acetal. When run with no lubrication or fluid of any kind, the life of both materials is determined by wear. When unlubricated, acetal against acetal wears faster than nylon against nylon. In some cases the best pair has been acetal against nylon, although no good theory has been developed to explain this.

It is customary to machine bearing or gear prototypes, and then use injection molding for production. When the application is severe or critical, care should be taken to ensure that the same grade of plastic is used for both machined and molded samples, and that processing is not sufficiently different to make extrapolation to molding an undue risk. Acetal resin is offered in extrusion and in molding types; they are chemically the same, but the extrusion type is of much higher molecular weight. It flows less readily than the injection-molding grade, and can be used to fill only simple cavities. Extrusion type is tougher (Izod impact 2.3 versus 1.4 for injection type) and has elongation 75 per cent versus 15 per cent. Tests of gears molded from each stock have shown that when lubricated, extrusion type will carry 25 per cent more load; when unlubricated, the two types of resin are about equal. Rod stock for machining prototypes is usually made from extrusion-type resin, and is often annealed before sale. In comparing molded gears with machined prototypes, severe applications should consider possible difference in behavior, or prototypes should be fabricated from the molding type of resin.

Dimensional Tolerances

Commercial molding of acetal resins will produce tolerances approaching those of Commercial Class gears. This means total composite error between .003 and .005 inch, and tooth-to-tooth composite error below .002 inch. In mechanical parts, the plastics industry makes a general distinction between "commercial molding" and "precision molding." In commercial molding, tolerance for acetal is usually $\pm.003$ inch for the first inch, and an additional $\pm.002$ inch for each additional inch. Precision molding tolerances may be $\pm.002$ for the first inch and less than $\pm.001$ inch for each additional inch. Precision molding presupposes that there are fewer cavities in the mold, all of similar geometry; that full runner system is put into the mold; and that at least one cavity is made as blank and filled with expected gate and molding cycle. Only after mold shrinkage is established in this way is the actual gear cavity cut. Precision tolerances cited above will be obtained only when the thickness of all sections of the gear is the same. If gears are large enough to make annealing advisable, the cavity sizing should be determined after annealing the piece from the blank cavity.

Plastics have greater coefficient of thermal expansion than metals, and the tolerance requested of molders should recognize this. Provision for expansion may be made in spacing of axes of gear train, or by increasing spacing between teeth. Running a plastic gear against a metal gear may help dissipate heat by conduction, and will also tend to reduce the total expansion as compared with an all-plastic gear train.

On the other hand, for light loads and speeds as in instrument gearing, plastic gears are employed because they operate smoothly with some interference, and thus have no backlash to cause loss of motion on starting or reversing direction of rotation.

Molding Considerations

Design for molding gears of acetal follows the normal practice of plastics. Even more than with metals, generous radii are recommended to prevent concentration of load stress. Radii and fillets will also improve filling of the cavity, which means better dimensional uniformity and reduction of molded-in stresses, which may cause warping of the gear or fracture of teeth under severe loading.

As molding makes practical a variety of cross-sections, it is usual practice to save material and molding cycle time by making the web thinner than hub or rim. To ensure adequate filling of cavity and minimal stress, axial thickness of web should at least equal radial thickness of rim below the tooth.

Radial thickness of rim should be at least three times the height from root to pitch circle of tooth. Hub outside diameter should be at least 1.5 times the shaft diameter. Hub length should not be less than shaft diameter.

Where thin web is employed, full advantage should *not* be taken of the speed with which acetal resins may be set up by running a very cold mold. The thin web will set first, and prevent contraction of the thicker rim. Tests have shown that an unannealed gear with thin web, running under severe load, may have such stresses molded in as to develop cracks from root of tooth through the rim.

Spokes or thick ribs in the web will cause the rim to shrink more opposite these sections. Large holes molded into the web of the gear will prevent shrinkage of the rim opposite the holes. In either case, gears will be out of round, and may not remain flat.

The cavity forming the gear and the pin forming the hub hole should be in the same half of the mold if concentricity is essential. In larger gears, gate should be located near center, or even made as diaphragm across hub hole.

In cutting cavities for gears, it has been the practice to use a gear shaper to make an internal ring gear, and to mount this between plates to form the molding cavity. The cavity is made oversize to allow for shrinkage due to thermal contraction or crystallization of plastic, and to relaxation of molding stresses. This shrinkage will pull the plastic from the periphery of the cavity, and result in a larger pressure angle on the molded gear teeth. The increase in pressure and backlash is small, and if gears are to mate with gears of similar diameter made in the same way, the pressure angles will match and perform well. When the plastic gear is to mate with a metal gear of standard pressure angle, it may be necessary to use a gear cutter of special shape in making the cavity.

Specification to Molder

The prospective user of plastic gears should provide his supplier with information needed to ensure satisfactory parts, both as to geometry of part and conditions of use. Many drawings will be based on practice with metals; these may not only prevent making the best part, but may also increase the cost of production.

Drawings should provide front and cross-section views of rim, web and hub, naming tolerances and fillet radii. If the web can be thickened, or mold parting line and gate are objectionable in an area, that should be so stated. Materials requested should be named as to generic type of plastic, and maker's type designation; if alternate or reworked materials are acceptable or to be negotiated, that should be part of specification request. The following should be supplied:

number of teeth	tooth-to-tooth error
diametral pitch	total tooth composite
nominal pitch diameter	error
pressure angle	concentricity
outside diameter	backlash

Conditions of use should be specified as completely as possible, to provide the supplier with information on dimensional problems which may arise in use. Not infrequently this will permit the molder or fabricator to recall experiences in a similar application. The intended use should be revealed, together with mating gear material, pitch diameter, and backlash expected on assembly. Operating loads, speeds, temperature and lubrication should be specified. Chemical and moisture environment should be defined.

Metal Inserts in Acetal Gears

Use of inserts generally increases the cost of a gear, but may provide advantages.

Knurled shafts are a common type of insert, eliminating

a fastening operation. Longitudinal grooves may be added to prevent rotation of the gear. Transverse grooves or shoulders will prevent axial movement; the technique is particularly useful with helical bevel or worm gears, in which rotation produces axial thrusts.

Stamped metal inserts are used where web must be thin, or where thermal expansion must be minimized. These may be metal discs with corrugations or holes near periphery, into which plastic may flow when a gear tooth tire is molded on. Similar inserts may be made from die-cast metals.

Metal inserts over 3 inches in diameter should be pre-heated above 250°F, to improve flow of plastic. Where possible, choice should be of inserts of high thermal expansion so that their contraction will relieve the stress imposed in the cooling plastic periphery.

Fastening Gears to Shafts

Internal splines may economically be molded into the hub of plastic gears. Torque capacity is high, but the cost of mating grooves in the shaft is relatively great, and the technique is not often used.

Knurled shafts may be pressed into molded gears, or used as inserts at time of molding. The knurled shaft will usually serve as its own broach. Torque capacity is fair, and technique is inexpensive.

Keys to join grooves in molded plastic hub and shaft are widely used. They permit good torque, ease of disassembly and moderate cost. Keys should have rounded edges to prevent stress concentration.

Integral shafts, molded as a single piece with gear, are the least expensive technique, and may also provide the bearing surface needed in assembly in metal housings.

Set screws provide only limited torque capacity, but are inexpensive. When disassembly must be repeated many times,

a metal insert in the plastic hub may be used. Self-tapping
screws of thread-cutting rather than thead-forming type are
preferable for torque and speed of use.

Gear Terminology

In order to use the later sections on design of gearing, the
following summary of gear terminology is given. Reference
should be made to Figure 5.1 as illustration of terms applied
to spur gears.

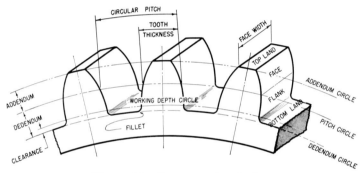

Figure 5.1. Spur gear terminology.

The smaller of two gears is usually called the pinion. Two
mating gears may be regarded as two friction wheels operating
at same peripheral speed, on the same center as the gears.
The point of contact of these wheels is the *pitch point*. The
distance from axis of one gear to the other is the center
distance. The *pitch circle* of each gear is the circle whose
diameter is the same as the respective friction wheel. It is
the circle described by the succession of contact points of the
rotating gears.

Circular pitch, P_c, is the distance measured along the
pitch circle from point on one tooth to corresponding point
on adjacent tooth of same gear. Circular pitch is given as
½ inch, 1¼ inch, etc.

Diametral pitch, P_d, is the number of teeth per inch of diameter of pitch circle. Diametral pitch is given as 4, 6, 16, etc. It is commonly used in commercial specification as pitch diameter and center distances can then be given in whole numbers.

Pitch diameter, D_p, is the diameter of the pitch circle.

The above terms are related by these equations:

$$P_d = \frac{\text{number of teeth in gear} \times P_c}{\pi} = \frac{\text{number of teeth}}{D_p} = \frac{\pi}{P_c}$$

Normally, it is desired that driven gears have constant angular displacement for increments of rotation of the driving gear. To achieve this, a variety of curvatures for profile of gear teeth could be used. In practice, the involute of a circle is used. The angle between the radius of the gear and the tangent of the involute base circle at the pitch point is called the *pressure angle.* American practice has standardized on pressure angles of 14.5° or 20°. The latter angle is also standardized in a shorter tooth form, called stub. The three forms are not interchangeable, and all gears or racks in the train must have the same pressure angle. For plastic gearing, the 20° pressure angle is preferred because it provides greater stiffness to individual teeth. However, the 14.5° angle is more widely used in plastics because metal gears are predominantly of 14.5° angle.

Backlash is the excess space at the pitch line between the teeth over the thickness of tooth of mating gear. The purpose of backlash is to prevent gears from making contact on both sides of the teeth. It must be provided for thermal expansion and for deviation in tooth geometry and mounting of gears. For gears operating at moderate loads and speeds, performance does not seem to be affected by reasonable variation in backlash.

TABLE 5.2. TOOTH FORM FACTOR. LOAD NEAR THE
PITCH POINT.

Number of Teeth	$14\frac{1}{2}°$	20° Full Depth	20° Stub
14	—	—	0.540
15	—	—	0.566
16	—	—	0.578
17	—	0.512	0.587
18	—	0.521	0.603
19	—	0.534	0.616
20	—	0.544	0.628
22	—	0.559	0.648
24	0.509	0.572	0.664
26	0.522	0.588	0.678
28	0.535	0.597	0.688
30	0.540	0.606	0.698
34	0.553	0.628	0.714
38	0.566	0.651	0.729
43	0.575	0.672	0.739
50	0.588	0.694	0.758
60	0.604	0.713	0.774
75	0.613	0.735	0.792
100	0.622	0.757	0.808
150	0.635	0.779	0.830
300	0.650	0.801	0.855
Rack	0.660	0.823	0.881

Using this method of determining tooth bending
stress two graphs (Figure 5.2 and Table 5.3) are presented showing the maximum recommended bending
stress for gears of "Delrin" and "Zytel." These graphs
apply only to molded and continuously lubricated gears.
To provide a margin of safety, the lines have been reduced 25 per cent below the lines which represent
average failure of the gears on test.

Design of Acetal Resin Gears

Much laboratory and practical data have been acquired
on gears of acetal resin, confirming the validity of designs
based on fatigue and wear data applied in the Lewis equation

as used for designing metal spur gears. This equation assumes that the entire load is carried by one tooth of each gear, in contact near the pitch point.

$$(A) \qquad S = \frac{F \times P_d}{f \times y}$$

$$(B) \qquad F = \frac{2T}{D_p}$$

where $S =$ bending stress, psi
$F =$ tangential force on tooth, pounds
$T =$ gear torque, pound per inch
$D_p =$ pitch diameter, inches
$f =$ gear face width, inches
$y =$ form factor from Table 5.2

Figure 5.2 shows maximum recommended bending stress for gears molded of "Delrin" 500 acetal resin, medium molecular weight, calculated from experience and the Lewis equation data. The graph applies only to molded and continuously lubricated gears. To provide a safety factor, the lines are drawn to stresses 25 per cent below data representing average failure points of test gears. Cycle life is here the total revolutions of the gear.

The above equation may be combined and modified with a design factor K, to provide the more useful forms:

$$(C) \qquad T = \frac{SD_p fyK}{2P_d}$$

and

$$(D) \qquad H = \frac{SD_p fnyK}{126,000P_d}$$

where $H =$ horsepower transmitted
$n =$ gear speed, rpm
$K =$ design factor from Table 5.3, accounting for conditions of lubrication, speed, mating steel gears, or high molecular weight acetal

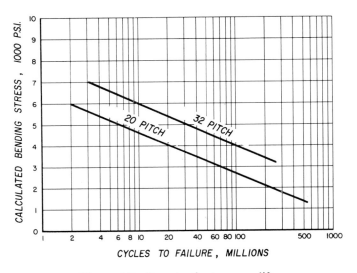

Figure 5.2. Gear tooth stress *vs.* life.

Sample problem:

What operating torque and what stall torque can be expected for molded gear 32 pitch, 20° full depth, 2.5 inch pitch diameter, 80 teeth, 0.5 inch face width? Gear is to operate at 2,000 rpm, average room temperature, initial lubrication, expected life 1,000 hours.

(1) The required cycle life is calculated
2,000 rpm $\times$ 1,000 hours $\times$ 60 min/hr = 120,000,000 cycles

(2) Pitch line velocity is calculated, to ensure it is within limits determined for K in Figure 5.2

$$V = \frac{\pi D_p n}{12 \text{ in./ft}} = \frac{\pi \times 2.5 \times 2,000}{12} = 1,310 \text{ ft per min}$$

(3) From Figure 5.2, the maximum recommended bending stress for 32 pitch gears at 120 million cycles is taken as 2,800

(4) K factor for design is taken as 0.72 from Table 5.3

(5) Form factor for tooth is taken from Table 5.2

(6) Substitution into Equation (C) is made, for T, gear torque under normal load

TABLE 5.3. VALUES OF DESIGN FACTOR *K*.
Values based on maximum pitch line velocity of 1,600 fpm.

Teeth	Material	Mating Gear Material	Lubrication *	Pitch	*K* Factor
Molded	500	500	Yes	20-32	1.00
Molded	500	500	No	20	0.45
Molded	500	500	No	32	0.80
Molded	100	100	Yes	20-32	1.40
Molded	100	100	No	20	0.50
Molded	100	Hob cut steel	Yes	20	1.2
Molded	100	Hob cut steel	No	20	.8

* Yes—refers to continuous lubrication.
No —refers to initial lubrication.

$$T = \frac{2,800 \times 2.5 \times 0.5 \times 0.74 \times 0.72}{2 \times 32} = 29.1 \text{ lb-in.}$$

(7) Torque at stall load can be determined from yield point stress at 75°F from Figure 2.11, using Equation C without design factor *K*

$$T \text{ at stall} = \frac{10,000 \times 2.5 \times 0.5 \times 0.74}{2 \times 32} = 145 \text{ lb-in.}$$

This value for stall torque is in good agreement with experience, which has shown that gears of acetal resin withstand stall loads which have been calculated to impose tooth stresses 3 or 4 times the yield point stress. Such loadings spread stress over several teeth, and safety factor is automatically introduced into calculation because Equation C is based on stress supported by a single tooth.

Acetal gearing is used where lack of stick-slip and minimal lubrication are important, as in high speed data indicator of Figure 5.3. Electrically actuated, the mechanism moves printed tape to viewing position. A major use is in airport control towers to provide immediate information on traffic and weather. Acetal parts include spur gear, helical gears, geneva gear and guide rollers. Rapid stop-and-start motion is essential, and helical acetal gear far outlasted steel

Figure 5.3. Data indicator.

gear working against same steel worm. Similarly, acetal outlasted bronze gears about four times. Application of Lewis
gear calculations (which are based on assumption of loading
on a single tooth) showed the acetal to be stressed well beyond recommended limits, so it is apparent that the resilience
of acetal spread the load over several teeth. This is advan-
tageous as it also minimizes stick-slip and backlash.

6. PIPING, PUMPS, VALVES, FITTINGS AND CONTAINERS

PIPING

The resistance of acetal resins to solvents and petroleum has indicated its suitability for many uses in liquid handling, although acetals are not recommended for strongly acid or alkaline solutions. Among thermoplastics, acetals provide the strongest material in terms of stress-rupture life and endurance to fatigue by pressure surges during pumping, along with high resistance to impact and abrasion, and retention of these properties over a wide range of temperature.

It is well-recognized that pipe of various plastics will fail by rupture under prolonged stress considerably below that which can be withstood for short times. Figure 6.1 plots hoop stress versus time for acetal pipe ("Delrin" 150, high molecular weight formaldehyde homopolymer) at three temperatures. Using the common Barlow formula the hoop stresses shown on right ordinate can be used to determine recommended continuous working pressure for any size pipe.

$$S = \frac{pD}{2t}$$

where S = long term working hoop stress in pounds per square inch
p = internal pressure, pounds per square inch
D = outside diameter, inch
t = wall thickness, inch

For example, the curve levels out at 3,000 psi hoop stress

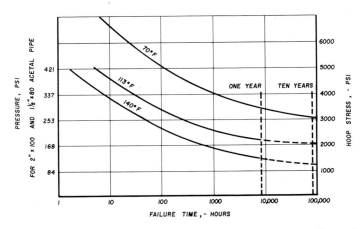

Figure 6.1. Stress rupture. Life data on acetal pipe. Effect of temperature (water-filled in water bath).

at 100,000 hours at 70°F. To determine recommended long-term working pressure for 0.100 wall 2-inch pipe:

$$3,000 = \frac{p \times 2.375}{2 \times .100}$$
$$p = 250 \text{ psi}$$

Life of more than 100,000 hours (11.4 years) should be expected with neutral water in pipe internally pressured at 250 psi. Field experience has shown excellent correlation with these curves under a variety of pressures, and it appears that sour crude petroleum and brine give essentially the same rupture life. In the presence of water, acetal, polyvinyl chloride ASTM type I, and acrylonitrile/butadiene/styrene type II are the strongest thermoplastic pipes. The vinyl and ABS materials lost about 50 per cent of their long-term strength (water method) when determinations were made in Texas sour crude oil.

Because of its high resistance to creep, acetal pipe does not normally balloon on pressure failure. In oil-field installations, where valves have been closed accidentally and pressure on 2″ x .100″ pipe rose to 1,000 psi, failure has been encountered only in one of the 20-foot lengths used to make up the line. Longer time failures are usually only at a tiny slit, which can be cut out and replaced with a heat-joined coupling. The mode of failure is important in a practical way, as experience to date indicates the rest of line is not impaired.

Resistance to cyclic surges of pumping is critical for many proposed uses of plastic piping. Acetal piping was subjected to 30 cycles per minute, each cycle consisting of ¾ second to reach peak, ¾ second at peak, ¼ second to drop to zero pressure and ¼ second at zero. As acetal resin shows quick recovery from stress, without loss of strength due to fatigue, the surge curve was 50 per cent higher than the control, as shown in Figure 6.2. An oil gathering line installation of acetal pipe still operated perfectly after three years of 55 surges per minute from zero to 150 psi, where fatigue had eliminated other plastics in a few weeks.

Tests of pressure loss due to frictional flow, over a range of flow rates, have been made on 1,000 feet of 1½-in. acetal pipe made as continuous length and a similar length of acetal pipe assembled from 20-foot lengths and joined couplings. Within the precision of measurement, the pressure loss was the same. Acetal pipe shows flow rates which indicate major operating advantage over metal pipe, due to internal smoothness and larger inside diameter for given outside size. Figure 6.3 shows that 2 x .100 inch acetal pipe (2.175 I.D.) has same pressure loss over range of flow rates as steel pipe of 2.500 inch I.D. Similar data show pressure loss in 1½-in. acetal pipe to be the same as for 2-in. steel pipe.

The above data and field experience with many miles of pipe in oil and brine service prove that acetal resins are

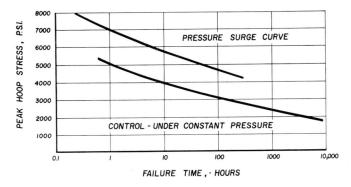

Figure 6.2. Surging and constant pressure *vs.* time to failure. Acetal pipe, water-filled, 113°F.

the first thermoplastic competition for steel or cement asbestos pipe under high sustained or surging pressure. In addition to the good performance, major savings are derived from lower installation cost. One man can easily carry five 20-foot lengths of 2-in. pipe (2⅜ in. outside diameter). Acetal pipe has good resistance to stringing across alkali flats and to soil burial. All such pipe has carbon black incorporated to provide resistance to sunlight. Pipe can be trenched as soon as joined; enough should be left out of the ditch to ensure that succeeding joints can be made without cocking when joined. Thermal expansion should be allowed for; if installed at −10°F to 40°F, little or no serpentine path need be made. If installed at 90°F, the center of the pipe should be deliberately displaced up to 18 in. from the ends. Installation in soil at 140°F should be with displacement up to 2 feet to allow contraction or distribution of stresses in cooling to around 0°F.

The highly crystalline acetals, with higher strength and fatigue endurance, present problems in extrusion of stress-free pipe of precise dimensions. Accordingly, the Du Pont

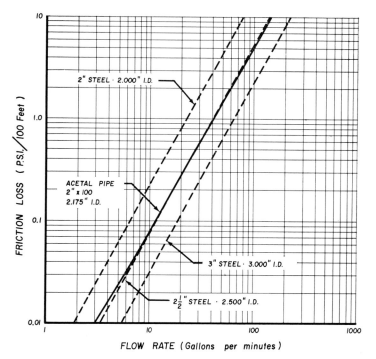

Figure 6.3. Acetal pipe 2 inch x 100 compared to steel pipe. Friction loss *vs.* flow rate for water @ 70°F.

Company is itself making and selling it under the name "Delrin" acetal resin pipe, and providing field technical men for installation assistance. Shorter lengths and tubing sizes below 0.5 inch are being made by custom and proprietary extruders using forming box, cold mandrel, or free-extrusion techniques.

Joining of Acetal Pipe

Plastic pipe is not usually joined by threaded fittings because the notch sensitivity of plastics requires thick walls to permit generously radiused threads. There may also be creep or relaxation at the joint or problems of thermal expansion to cause stress concentration. It has been customary to join plastic pipe by solvents or adhesives. For acetal resin this is not practical because of its resistance to solvents.

Joining by heat is practical for pipe and fittings of acetal. This is done by melting a thin layer of each surface to be mated, i.e., end of pipe and molded socket coupling, then inserting the pipe into the coupling by hand pressure and holding until freezing occurs. The integral joint is composed entirely of acetal resin and is achieved in a 25-second cycle. Under field conditions, a crew of three men can assemble 2-in. pipe at rate of 500 to 800 feet per hour, using an electrically heated tool and a portable alternating current generator. A joint made this way is considerably stronger than the pipe itself under tensile and bending stresses, and about as good under impact of falling objects. Full pressure may be exerted on such joints as soon as 5 minutes after making the last joint.

Equipment and Technique. (1) *Cutting pipe.* The pipe must be perpendicular to axis in order to get rapid and strong joint. Hacksaw and miter box are satisfactory; so also is a cutter as used for brass or aluminum tubing. Shavings and burrs should be removed with a knife or file to permit seating in the joining tool.

(2) *Chamferring pipe.* This is done around outside of the leading end to provide a reservoir for molten resin. The joint is an interference fit and hence a small amount of resin is built up around the inside of coupling when the molten end of the pipe is pushed into a coupling, or other fitting. The chamfer assists insertion into heating tool, and provides a reservoir for a ring of flash so there is no restriction of flow through the pipe. For 2-inch pipe, chamfer is 20° from axis,

⅜ inch long. Chamfering tool is like a pipe-threader, with tubular sleeve to center blades on pipe. In nominal 2-in. size, the pipe has an outside diameter of $2.375 \pm .010$ inch; the coupling has a constant inside diameter (except for center portion of smaller diameter against which pipe seats) of $2.360 + .005, \ -.003$ inch.

(3) *Cold ring* (Figure 6.4). This is a split-ring steel clamp, with two functions. It is clamped around the pipe ¾ inch from the end, and may be set by reference to plugs ¾ in. thick on the heating tool. The cold ring, with toggle clamp to grip the pipe tightly, ensures roundness of the pipe when pushed into joining tool, keeps to hold the joining tool perpendicular to the pipe, and shows how far the coupling should be pushed on after heating.

(4) *Joining tool* (Figure 6.5). A joining tool is an aluminum block in which are two 400-watt heaters and ther-

Figure 6.4. Cold ring for pipe joining.

Figure 6.5. Electrically heated joining tool for pipe and coupling.

mal switch; on one side is a plug die to heat the inside of the
coupling; on the other side is a ring die to heat the outside
of the pipe. An indicator light in an insulated handle shows
when the heater is drawing current. The unit operates effi-
ciently in the field from a portable 1,000-watt alternating
current generator. The tool surface reaches 550°F, and
should occasionally be checked with a temperature crayon
or thermocouple. Above 570°F degradation may occur faster
than the joint can be made, resulting in brittle or weak joints.
Pipe and coupling are pushed into dies, the coupling 5 to 10
seconds before the pipe, and the tool may be rotated against
them to ensure good contact. When the pipe has advanced
to the cold ring and the coupling has advanced to the center
plate, they should be removed axially and quickly pushed
together. The joint is held by hand pressure for 10 seconds.
Axial removal is important to avoid smearing dies and to

prevent molten resin from adhering to them. The dies are coated with polytetrafluoroethylene to minimize sticking; over 3,000 joints can be made without appreciable wear of coating.

When acetal pipe is to be tied into an existing steel line, a "maintenance" joint is used. A flange end molded of acetal is joined to the acetal pipe. This is then bolted with gaskets to the steel pipe flange.

Liquid-tight joints in acetal piping can be made with metal clamp type fittings used for soft metal pipe. Care should be taken that metal parts do not have burrs which may cut the plastic.

PUMPS

Pumps with parts of acetal are used for coolants, lubricants and in general purpose handling of farm chemicals. For hydrolysis reasons, continuous water service is not recommended above 150°F, although brief operation has been satisfactory at 200°F. Pumps require many of the properties of the acetal resins: stiffness, tensile strength, dimensional stability, and resistance to corrosion, abrasion, creep, and fatigue of pressure cycling. Major achievements have not been made by simple substitution of acetal for metal, but by re-design of parts so as to take advantage of acetal bearing surfaces and inherent economies of injection molding.

A good example is the gear pump of Figure 6.6. Here the switch from brass to acetal brought higher efficiency to the gear mesh because of resilience and low friction of acetal. Operating *PV* (see Chapter 4) is in range from 200 to 500, well within design limits. Horsepower was halved, and water pumped at 5 gallons per minute rose 12°F with acetal, 75°F with brass. Oil pumped at 7.5 gallons per minute rose 45°F with acetal and 103°F with brass. The only lubricant for acetal was the liquid being pumped; hence contamination

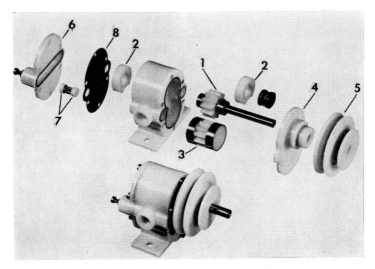

Figure 6.6. Gear pump with variable by-pass.

and grease fittings are avoided. No fall-off in developed head was noted in over 2,000 hours and wear was negligible in over 500 million cycles. The numbers of following paragraphs refer to part numbers of Figure 6.6.

(1) Drive gear, molded of acetal directly onto stainless steel drive shaft. Sleeve bearings 0.04 in. thick, of metal specified for the use, are slipped over bosses molded each side of gear.

(2) Bushings of acetal are slipped over the metal sleeve bearings, providing acetal-metal-acetal bearings. The bushings do not rotate, and fit tightly into the figure-eight cavity of the pump body. Friction parts are thus replaceable without damage to the body.

(3) Idler gear of acetal has a large bushing on each side of the pumping face of the gear. Metal sleeves fit over these bushings, and in turn fit into the lower portion of the cavity

of the pump body. These bushings also make an integral
seal at the end of the gear face. The metal sleeves provide the
advisable dissimilar material for bearing surface; the fluid
being pumped provides separation between faces of acetal
gears. In normal and in abrasive service, acetal gears have
shown longer life than metal gears.

(4) Front cover of acetal is molded with precision boss
extension, containing a hole for the drive shaft and its carbon-
ceramic mechanical seal. This boss absorbs side-loading of
the shaft and distributes it over a large area.

(5) Drive sheave of acetal is mounted on ball bearing,
whose inside race fits tightly to the outside of the front cover
boss. The sheave is held to the flat of the drive shaft by a
star ring of 300 inch-pound torque.

(6) Rear cover of acetal has a molded-in by-pass cavity
and boss for an adjusting screw.

(7) Acetal buttons control by-pass flow by spring separation, which is adjusted by external screw.

(8) Cover is stamped from 0.042-inch stainless steel and
is the most economical way to seal by-pass channel. For
corrosive services, a stainless steel insert can be used in
pump cavity.

Volute pumps are also made with acetal resin, one example being that of Figure 6.7. This use may reach 21 stages
for deep wells. Acetal has low friction, resistance to
abrasion and build-up of mineral deposits, as occurs when
brass impellers are used in water containing iron. Creep
resistance is vital, as bowls are clamped under steel straps
at 3,000 psi to prevent interstage leakage. The volute is
molded with projecting studs, and the face plate has matching holes. The impeller is formed by registering studs in
holes, then joining the two moldings by cold-heading the
studs, similar to parts shown in Figure 6.8.

Thread strength of acetal was found to permit savings

Figure 6.7. Multi-stage deep well volute pump.

in weight and manufacturing costs in the impeller of other jet
well pumps. The usual practice in adapting plastics to impellers has been to use a threaded brass insert, pressed or
molded into the hub, to take the torque of starting. It has
been found that threads molded of acetal readily withstood
these stresses. Figure 6.8 shows an impeller molded as two
parts, and studs on one are fitted through holes in the other.

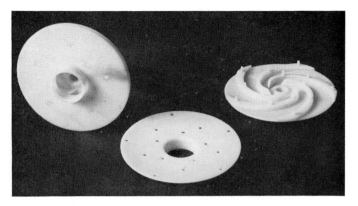

Figure 6.8.   Impeller showing studs to be headed over face plate.

By manual arbor press, a load is applied in excess of compressive yield strength (17,000 psi) and the material is compressed to lock the parts together. Using this technique, one operator can assemble over 200 impellers per hour.

Molded acetal parts comprise the pumping chamber and housing for the high vacuum hand pump pictured in Figure 6.9. This is a diaphragm pump used for alcohols, esters, aromatic and petroleum solvents. Most of these pumps are used on farms to remove gasoline from drums; hence weatherability and impact strength over a range of temperatures are needed.

The marine bilge pump in Figure 6.10 uses molded acetal for impeller, volute, motor cover, inlet plate and screen support. Acetal resists abrasion and corrosion of salt water. Resiliency of the material provides unique assembly techniques, which permit easy servicing. The motor cover is attached to the volute by a double snap-fit, forming a watertight seal with an O-ring. The pump impeller has a molded-in shoulder on its inner diameter which snaps into a recessed

Figure 6.9. Housing and valves for diaphragm
pump.

groove on the shaft. Although normal use is a five-minute
on-and-off cycle, the pump has run successfully in continuous
service where motor temperatures reached 275°F and under-
the-cover temperature was 200°F.

The simple hand-operated spray gun of Figure 6.11 uses
molded acetal parts for low friction and resistance to

Figure 6.10. Bilge pump.

agricultural and insecticidal solutions and dispersions. The gun is made with an adapter to fit directly to original package cans. The nozzle has an intricate spiral path, and can be adjusted from fog to steady stream. O-rings seal the piston; acetal is important in providing long life to the seal because of absence of stick-slip with variety of fluids. The parts require no finishing after molding, and are less costly than brass which is the only other satisfactory material.

VALVES

A novel design for foot and check valves using a molded acetal part to guide and retain the valve seat is shown in

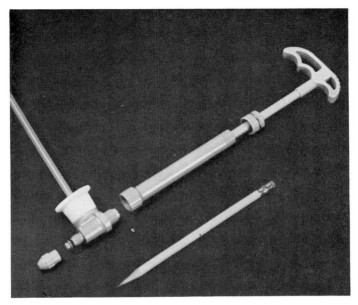

Figure 6.11. Hand spray gun.

Figure 6.12. Here the legs of acetal center the seat, and after 1.5 million cycles showed no wear. The seat is fastened to the guide with an 8-32 self-tapping screw; it showed no loosening over 1.5 million cycles, up to 180°F in gasoline, or in water thermal shocks from 180 to 32°F.

Valves, spray heads and control knobs are molded of acetal resin for pressure-dispensing packages such as aerosol insecticides and shave cream. Acetal is little affected dimensionally or strengthwise by essential oils or propellants, and injection molding produces parts of excellent uniformity and gloss. In many aerosol valves nylon or polyolefins can be used as there is no need for easy relative motion of parts within the valve. However, one design requires acetal for its dimensional

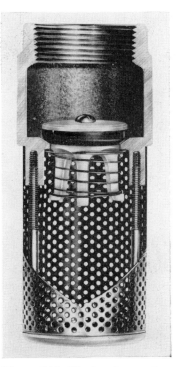

Figure 6.12. Check valve seating
guide.

stability and absence of stick-slip. Figure 6.13 shows a valve
with slider of acetal which selects one of a pair of ports, and
provides aerosol spray whether can is upright or inverted.

Many plumbing parts are being changed from brass castings
to injection-molded acetal for corrosion resistance, cost
saving, and because little or no finishing is required of the
plastic piece upon removal from the mold. Acetal is used
because of dimensional stability and strength of threads. A

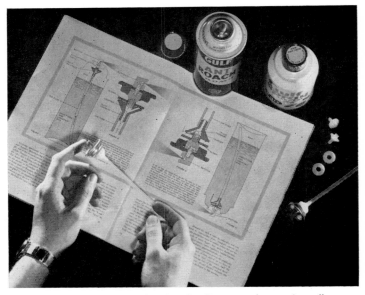

Figure 6.13. Aerosol valve for "erect or inverted use."

good example is in Figure 6.14, which shows a toilet inlet valve bonnet and ferrule to adapt the assembly to the bottom of the tank.

FITTINGS

Many parts in fluid-handling systems have remained in brass because of need for thread-strength and resistance to creep. As cost of metals and their finishing has risen, newer high-strength plastics have become attractive for some types of fittings.

Pipe plugs are such a use, requiring strength against stripping of threads, yet resilience to provide a liquid seal. Pipe plugs molded of acetal are being used to protect fixtures

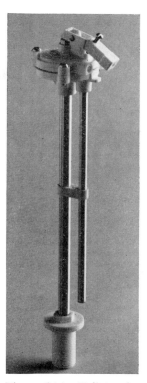

Figure 6.14. Toilet valve
bonnet and base ferrule.

in shipment, to plug pipe ends, or as non-sticking stoppers for
fill- and drain-openings in small gasoline engines, power steering and power brake systems.

Couplings, elbows, manifolds and valve seats used to mix a
variety of beverage syrups and water are molded of acetal,
which does not alter, nor is it affected by, concentrated
flavorings.

Garden hose couplings are a proven use for acetal, because of strength of thread, resistance to abrasion, and essential absence of creep due to expansion ferrule. A variety of lawn sprinkler designs use acetal for thread strength, and dimensional stability and stiffness in actuating levers and gears.

Showerheads largely or entirely molded of acetal are being marketed by several companies. As they come from the mold, parts do not require finishing or threading before assembly. They have high thread-strength, do not corrode and show less depositing of salts from hard water. Dimensional stability is good, and adjustments are easily made.

A different type of fitting is a shock absorber for home water systems. This is a cylindrical unit containing an elastomer diaphragm. The unit is fitted as close to fixture valve as possible, and water hammer expands the diaphragm against an air cushion between it and the housing. Acetal resin was chosen for its thread-and burst-strength and resistance to hot water service.

CONTAINERS

Plastics are used to make containers, or to coat containers made of other materials where flexibility, transparency, toughness, or special chemical resistance is needed. Such uses are ethylene squeeze bottles, styrene pill bottles, plasticized vinyl jackets on glass bottles, and corrosion-resistant linings for cans and tanks. Present acetal resins do not have these degrees of flexibility or transparency, nor are solutions readily made for coating; hence acetals are not adaptable to general container usage.

In permeability, acetal and polyethylene are complementary. Common gases, such as air and carbon dioxide, pass through polyethylene about 15 times faster than through acetal. Water and ethyl alcohol vapors pass through acetal about fifteen times faster than through polyethylene. Acetal has low permeability to hydrocarbons, essential oils, and fluorocarbons used as propellants in aerosols. Chemical and permeability data are in Tables 2.1, 2.3, 2.4 and 2.5.

Containers made of acetal are used for pressure-dispensed aerosol perfumes and room deodorizers. Impact toughness over range of temperature is needed, as well as attractive appearance for carrying in purse. Some are blow-molded in one piece, using techniques and equipment as for polyethylene bottles. Valves and nozzles may be fitted by spin joining or by crimping a decorative metal cap around head and gasket. Molded dimensions are less variable than those of blown glass bottles.

Some acetal aerosol bottles are molded as two pieces, with upper and lower halves joined by spin joining. This technique permits two-colored bottles, or economical molding of relief designs on each half. Flash at outside of joint is easily removed by passing the joined bottle through a sizing ring. In production, incidence of leakage at the joint has been less than with metal cans.

Purse-size aerosol containers have top or bottom integrally molded with essentially cylindrical sides. The remaining end is spin-joined after filling with refrigerated liquid charge. Spin joining heats only the interface to be joined, hence does not volatilize the charge. Because of wiping and heating action of spin joining operation, it is not necessary to remove spilled charge from interface before joining.

7. HARDWARE AND FASTENERS

Hardware is a miscellaneous category. This chapter discusses acetal moldings, mostly small, which may or may not be designed as components for a single end-use. Additional examples of hardware designed especially for an end-use appear in Chapter 6, Section D: Fittings for Fluid Handling; Chapter 8: Automotive; and Chapter 9: Appliance and Electrical. Many of the items summarized in this chapter are fastening devices which depend on stiffness, resilience, or resistance to creep to achieve results not usually obtained with plastics.

Builders Hardware

Although the construction industry generally recognizes this item, it is difficult to define more closely than to say it comprises items for doors, windows and other building usage, aside from plumbing and electrical. This has become an attractive field for plastics in view of the rising price of metal parts and the increasing desire of the public for color. Most of the parts which use acetal depend on good abrasion and bearing qualities.

Rollers for sliding doors and cabinet drawers are one of the earliest examples of acetal use. Unlike steel, they do not gall aluminum track. Particularly at high humidities, acetal shows less tendency than nylon to develop flat spots on prolonged static load. The absence of stick-slip friction is important in assuring that these rollers rotate rather than skid.

Some of these rollers are press-fitted around a ball-bearing insert.

Door knobs for several makers of quality hardware are molded in acetal for variety of color and texture, resistance to abrasion and freedom from tarnish. Some are molded in two pieces, with the knob as a cup and the separate cover plate snapped into undercut on the inner diameter of the cup. These assemblies appear to be of one piece, because of the tight fit. The ability of acetal to hold set screw to shaft, or to be press-fitted onto shaft, has brought neat, economical assembly.

Lock sets with rotating parts of acetal, lubricated only initially, have shown greater life than cast brass or steel. As might be expected, a combination of nylon and acetal gives longest life.

In spring-counterbalanced double-hung window sash, acetal bushings are used to support the spiral which winds the spring. Acetal here must perform as a bearing in dusty and humid air.

For dimensional stability and retention of thread position, acetal is used in pneumatic door closer end caps, adjusting valves and hinge bushings.

Furniture

Casters are molded of acetal, to provide bearing surface for steel axle, and resistance to flattening under prolonged loading. Acetal bushings are also molded to lock the metal shaft of a caster into the socket, and to reduce the likelihood of splitting of wooden legs.

Threaded Fasteners

Bolts and nuts molded of acetal show good retention of threads under pull-out and vibration tests. Inserts of acetal are used to make metal nuts of the self-locking or vibration-resistant type. Nuts molded of acetal are used in lawn furniture because thread strength is better than with aluminum, galvanic corrosion of dissimilar metals is avoided, and strength is retained when wet. In auto and appliance assemblies, acetal nuts or bolts may be preferred to other plastics because of resistance to paint solvents and baking temperatures. It should be remembered that stresses may be high in threaded parts, particularly at elevated temperatures. Before parts are subjected to metal-treating solutions, it should be determined that acid conditions will not cause splitting or crazing of highly-stressed acetal parts. Whitworth or threads with rounded root are preferred as providing less opportunity for stress concentration.

When bolts are molded in split molds (where the molded piece is not unscrewed from the cavity) the flash is usually less than with nylon or styrene. Internally threaded nuts should be unscrewed—not bumped—from the mold, as threads will usually be deformed if forced from the mold pin. Except for very small parts, if mating is desired with standard metal threads, the mold for acetal should not be made with standard-thread taps and dies because of the need to allow for mold shrinkage.

Clips and Snap-fit Fasteners

Resistance to fatigue, and speedy return to shape after deformation, have put acetal into many fasteners using snap-action. One is the cabinet latch of Figure 7.1. It is snapped into the opening of a steel cabinet and held by the finger outside the main frame of the molding. The knob (here shown without the door through which it is inserted) is retained by the snap-action of its stud in the fingers of the center portion of the latch. This design accepts as much as ⅛ inch misalignment between door and cabinet.

Figure 7.1.—Spring-action cabinet latch.

Similar clips may be used to hold decorative trim strips and name plates on appliances and autos.

Snap-action and resistance to creep permitted new design of an adjustable support for shelving, shown in Figure 7.2. The track strip is injection-molded in lengths of 12 and 24 inches, and is competitive in price with stamped metal track. Shelves may be moved up or down by pushing in the projecting studs, without need to remove shelf from cabinet. Acetal exceeded all other tough plastics in resistance to creep from the long-time loading of this application.

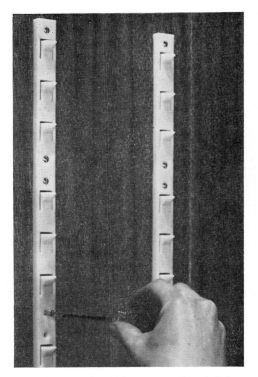

Figure 7.2. Adjustable support for shelving.

Another use of the spring action of acetal is in "memory fingers" which show maximum deflection of an instrument pointer. An established use is on a torque wrench, where molded-in spring action makes the legs of the finger grip the track along the edge of the dial. As the indicating pointer moves along the dial, it pushes the memory finger ahead; when the torque pointer returns to zero, the memory finger shows maximum deflection of the pointer. In this case, acetal's resistance to fatigue and temperature extremes, coupled with low coefficient of friction, provided a simple answer to a long-felt need.

Split coolets of acetal are used in small tool holders. Toughness, resistance to creep, and dimensional stability when wet put acetal into a collet for joining fishing rod to handle, as shown in Figure 7.3. Here the collet is pressed around

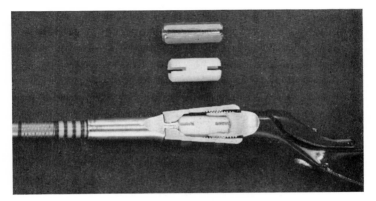

Figure 7.3. Fishing rod collet.

knurled shaft; threaded ferrule is screwed around the collar to make a vibration-proof joint, which is easily taken apart without tools.

Clothing Fasteners

Acetal is not adversely affected by dry-cleaning solvents, detergents, or washing and drying temperatures. While nylon has been used in many clothing fitments, acetal has been found preferable in some because of better retention of stiffness and dimensions when wet. Examples of use are slider and teeth for zippers, snap fasteners, and buckles and strap adjusting slides for underwear.

8. AUTOMOTIVE INDUSTRY

The automotive industry quickly became a major market for acetal resin, because production volume justifies injection molding, with its attendant design versatility and economy, and the engineering atmosphere is imaginative. The summary of actual uses in this chapter is grouped under headings of the chapters which have discussed material properties, i.e., Bearings, Gears, Fluid Handling, and a selection of uses specific to the auto industry. These uses warrant study by designers not in the auto industry because they show unusual answers to problems which are not unique to the auto industry.

Bearings

Considering the haphazard maintenance given most automobiles, acetal bearings are attractive for compatibility (anti-score properties on metal shafts), conformability (to compensate for misalignment), embeddability (to absorb dirt), corrosion resistance (toward aromatic or oxidized fuel and lubricants, paint and adhesive solvents, ice melting compounds and antifreeze), and fatigue resistance (especially to eccentric loading or impact).

Loadings on acetal bearings range from speedometer pivots to spring shackle bushings in huge trailers; from simple pulleys for cords in radio tuners to steering column bushings and ball-seat steering joints. In all cases, parts are made by injection molding, and usually require no subsequent finishing operation. Tubing extruded from acetal is used as low-friction liner for conduit for flexible shafting used to drive speedometers.

Pulleys for parking brake cables are one of the earliest auto uses of acetal. These were formerly made by crimping or spot-welding together two metal stampings. The one-piece molded acetal part is cheaper and eliminates pinching of the cable, which occurred when the drawn cable wedged apart the halves of the metal pulley. The acetal pulley rotates freely without lubricant, does not develop flat spots when cable is pulled tight for long times, and does not deform at temperature of 220°F, which may be reached during baking of paint or when parked in tropic sun.

Many automotive bearings are for sliding use or for oscillation through a short arc rather than for continual rotation. Bearings which operate only through a small arc are used in clutch and brake pedal pivots, where lubrication can be infrequent. Low rotational speeds but eccentric loadings are applied to window regulator shafts and knobs. Figure 8.1

Figure 8.1. Steering knuckle bushings.

shows an acetal steering knuckle bushing as molded, and be-
hind it the bronze bushing which was replaced. Slots are for
lubricant distribution. The slit in the bushing is to ease the
critical tolerance requirements as to thermal expansion and to
facilitate assembly.

Bearings of acetal resin differ from most in that the coefficient of friction against steel is the same in starting to move
(static coefficient) as after motion has started (dynamic coefficient). This is spoken of as absence of "stick-slip" behavior, and is important when there is frequent starting or
reversal of direction. One example is the ball-seat in many
lubricated-for-life steering linkages shown in Figure 8.2.
Static and dynamic coefficients had to be alike in order to give

Figure 8.2. Steering link ball seat.

constant feel to steering. Acetal was selected because of the need for toughness, but small expansion from 0 to 100 per cent humidity, resistance to lubricant, and to creep under continuous load plus thousands of impact loadings.

One of the most used power brake systems uses six critical parts of acetal in the vacuum chamber illustrated in Figure 8.3. Two small bushings around center shaft hold it in sliding alignment. Bellows retainer and filter retainer (at top of picture) must have creep resistance after snap-fitting together. The seal retainer (white part at bottom) is molded of two pieces which are hot-peened together to hold rubber seal against shaft.

Where torque and eccentric loadings are difficult to predict,

Figure 8.3. Vacuum chamber of power brake.

testing of prototypes is the only way to select the best material. An example is a six-way power seat which uses acetal and nylon where each performs best. Threaded steel shafts rotate inside acetal nuts, and as each nut moves along axis it changes location or angle of back or seat. Acetal is used for nuts because of thread strength. Nylon is used for added toughness in the transmission gears and in dog stops to prevent jamming at end of run. Although the parts are small, they permitted reduction of manufacturing cost by four dollars as compared with all-metal assembly, and make the unit quieter in use.

Gears

For many gear uses (particularly with the variable alignment and loadings in automotive use) it is not possible to predict whether acetal, nylon, polycarbonate or ABS resin will be best considering performance and economics. If the load is such that lubrication is needed, the choice narrows to acetal and nylon. Speedometer drive gears have for over a decade been in nylon. Some have switched to acetal, but most remain in nylon. Choice is sometimes on assembly technique rather than on gear performance. If thread strength to bind to shaft is critical, acetal may be the choice. If stall torque is criterion, acetal is usually chosen because it is stiffer. If impact is severe, nylon may be preferred.

One gear use in farm machinery is a sprocket used in corn planter, Figure 8.4. The internal splines key it to the shaft along which it slides. Abrasion resistance in dust made acetal outlast cast iron in this use. Note the radius from spline into hub. A potential source of troublesome stress concentration was removed by this indentation of spline, and torque to failure was raised from 40 to over 90 foot pounds by this radius. The gear is three inches in diameter.

Figure 8.4. Corn planter sprocket.

Fluid Handling

Pipe or tubing of acetal has not been used commercially
in cars for carrying air, fuel or oil. Creep resistance is good
with flared fittings, but stiffness is such that kinking at bends
is more likely than with other plastic tubing.

Fittings in wide variety are molded from acetal. A radiator
cap knob conducts heat less than metal cap, and on partial
rotation diverts pressure to overflow line before removal.
Economical threaded caps and plugs are used for steering
and brake reservoirs and do not "freeze" to metal housing.

Vacuum brake check valves and bodies for windshield
washer pumps are commercial, and rely on good bearing
surface and dimensional stability.

Nearly all the outstanding properties of acetal are used
in the automatic control lubricator for vehicles, Figure 8.5.
The system uses engine oil pressure to develop 150 psi in a

Figure 8.5. Automatic central lubricator.

pump housing and via piston to move metered lubricant to chassis points. Body and fittings maintain tight fit on tubing despite engine compartment temperature of 250°F and vibration. The low coefficient of friction of the acetal cylinder walls permits nitrile rubber piston cap to move without stick-slip and to have long life.

General Automotive Uses

Attractive styling and savings in weight and costs are of major importance in design for compact cars. The 1960 and 1961 Valiant cars use instrument clusters, Figure 8.6, molded of acetal resin. This is a functional piece, from which hang the dash instruments and controls for transmission and heater. The acetal molding has no metal or fiber reinforcement. Molded-in bosses accept self-tapping screws for mounting and the installation is by conventional assembly techniques. The acrylic dial faces are fastened into the central opening by self-tapping screws directly to acetal; the similar thermal expansion of the two plastics puts less stress on acrylic pieces than does the traditional metal cluster housing.

The part in acetal weighs 2 pounds, a saving of 78 per cent of the weight of the 9 pound zinc casting of same size. There is no sacrifice in part performance. Dimensional stability is more than adequate for tight fit over range of temperature and humidity. Parts are molded in uncolored resin and painted to match car interior.

Figure 8.6. Instrument cluster housing.

There are considerable implications here for replacing the maze of wiring under an auto dash by circuits printed on back of housing, and rattle-free snap-in replacement of individual instruments.

Other housings come to mind where there is need for stiffness and resistance to engine-compartment fumes and temperature. Developments now in progress show promise for filter housings for air, fuel and oil; carburetor bowls and venturis less subject to erosion and corrosion which change metering action; heater ducts with molded-in studs for control surfaces.

Automobile knobs and handles have performed well in a variety of plastics. These are frequently molded over a metal insert to accept threaded or impaled shaft. Acetal presently seems justified only where savings can be made in size of insert, as parking brake handle. However, for such a simple use as gear shift knob acetal is used; molded-in threads are strong enough. The slightly soapy feel is prized by sports car drivers whose hands are often on the shift knob.

For window cranks, acetal has proven to have adequate stiffness and toughness in dimensions like those of traditional metal handles. Savings are possible because metal bearings can be eliminated, but so long as styling preference is for chrome surfaces it does not appear that acetal will displace zinc castings.

For many automotive electric parts a number of plastics can be used, and choice is usually based on price. One example of best-economy from the presently more expensive acetal is the socket for new baseless bulbs now used with printed circuit in dash and radio lighting. Heat resistance is needed, for the bulb is in contact with the socket. Creep resistance is needed to keep contacts against leads projecting from the bulb. Resilience must be adequate to accommodate large tolerances in glass envelope and printed circuit boards. Weight and volume must be small in order to impose little stress on the printed circuitry.

Fan blades and squirrel-cage blower wheels for heaters are molded of acetal for stiffness and dimensional stability. One is pictured in Figure 9.2.

9. APPLIANCES, BUSINESS MACHINES, AND ELECTRICAL APPARATUS

Putting these industries into a single chapter is practical because their use of acetal is in housings, in linkages to transmit or guide mechanical movements, and in some electrical control items. With but very few exceptions, acetal is used for mechanical rather than electrical properties. Present compositions of acetal are not self-extinguishing, but slow-burning (at same rate as for acrylics, styrene and co-polymers). Accordingly, acetal is not normally considered for support of current-carrying parts, as defined by Underwriters' Laboratories, Inc., and designers of appliances and of business machines use the same criteria for service and safety.

The appliance industry rapidly became a large market for acetal, because high volume justifies use of injection molds. Redesign with this new material often permits combining functions of several metal parts to improve performance and cost. The variety of domestic and industrial equipment using parts of acetal is so great that discussion in this chapter is by function rather than by type of equipment of which acetal is a component. This also permits the reader to turn from design chapters (Properties, Bearings, Gears) to discussion of actual uses in this chapter and in the Appendix.

Bearings

Acetal bearings are used from light loads, as in watt-hour meters, electric shavers and typewriters, to heavier loads and corrosive conditions as in washing machine wringers. In movie cameras and slide projectors acetal is used for ability to operate with only initial lubrication, similar coefficients for starting and running friction, quietness, and ability to absorb some vibration. Loads are usually well within recommended *PV* limits. An interesting example is the clothes-dryer drum bearing shown in Figure 4.17, where ability to operate at high temperatures is necessary.

Gears

Molded acetal gears are used in appliance timers, adding machines, clocks, electric can openers, hand and electric food mixers, postage meters, tape recorders, telephones and vending machines. None of these uses is sufficiently complex to warrant an illustration to indicate a novel design.

In an electric floor scrubber and polisher, a plastic gear was desired to reduce danger of current leak from motor to wet floor. Acetal was preferred for fatigue resistance and dimensional stability when wet.

Closely related to gears are printing wheels for calculators and indicator wheels for counters, since they are usually rotated by an integrally molded gear configuration. Acetal has rapidly moved into this use because of resistance to ink solvents, abrasion, and to flattening by millions of impressions.

General Appliance Components

Knobs and handles are molded from acetal where special needs must be met, as controls for steam irons. An interesting handle is the twist-top control for a sink garbage disposer, in Figure 9.1. Here the acetal replaced cast metal at a saving. The users like it because it is more comfortable to touch

Figure 9.1. Control for garbage disposer.

after exposure to hot water, does not chip, dent or scratch sink surfaces when dropped, and operates easily due to its good anti-friction properties.

Fluid Handling

Valve bodies for water softeners are molded in acetal. Evaluations are well along on use of acetal for pumps in clothes and dish washers.

Blower wheels for movie projectors, kitchen ventilators, hair dryers, dish washers, and auto heaters and defrosters are a good example of use of acetal for stiffness at elevated temperature and under centrifugal loadings. Typical shapes are in Figure 9.2. Stamped metal is replaced at lower cost, and smooth surfaces deliver up to 20 per cent more efficiency.

Electrical

Bobbins and coil forms use acetal where flanges of high stiffness are needed over range of temperature and humidity.

Figure 9.2. Blower wheels.

Present acetals cannot so readily be molded into thin sections as nylon or styrene.

Switches use acetal for mechanical parts when smooth operation is needed without lubricant. One use is as plunger to actuate safety cut-off switch when an access door is opened. Another use is a Navy rotary wafer switch over which a contact arm slides; acetal replaced laminated phenolic because of better dimensional stability and freedom from tracking after an arc.

Snap-action and stiffness are usual reasons for acetal in electrical parts. Sockets for baseless miniature bulbs are mentioned in Chapter 8. The resistance to fatigue put acetal into use as nonconducting spring in the switch of Figure 9.3.

Figure 9.3. Spring to ensure action of
switch.

A dramatic use of acetal is for the two halves of the arc
chute in load break distribution cut-out of Figure 9.4, seen as
a grid at top of picture. The device is mounted on utility pole
and opened and closed by lineman using standard hook and
handpole. Load is broken by pulling blade (hinged at
bottom) away from contact and out through the chute. The
normal arc is extinguished in a tenth of a second by the de-
ionizing gas generated by heat of arc. No fuse link or other
replaceable part or gas bottle is needed. Units have been used
200 times with uniform behavior, breaking 200 amperes at
15,000 volts and power factor over 70 per cent. At the end

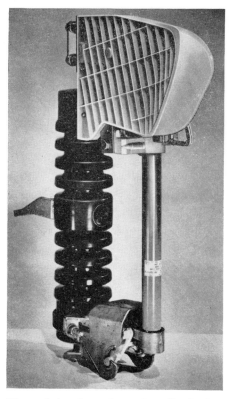

Figure 9.4.   Arc chute for distribution
load cut-out.

of this test period the chute showed almost no wear, only
very slight discoloration, and no evidence of carbon tracking.
Acetal was chosen because of good arc behavior, stiffness,
toughness over range of humidity and temperature, and because soot, fog and ice do not adhere strongly.

Appendix

COMMERCIAL USES OF ACETAL RESIN

This listing is of some of the commercial uses, selection being made only of items which indicate a general utility. To keep the list brief, items have been named in only one place. For instance, under "Electrical" the listing is of those uses where the acetal is intimately related to the electrical mechanism. An electric appliance using acetal as a bearing in its mechanical operation would be listed under "Bearings." Groupings here follow Chapter headings; some uses are discussed in the text, and may be located from the index. It should be emphasized that where the acetal has replaced an older material, redesign of part or processing technique was frequently adopted.

BEARINGS AND WHEELS

	Material Replaced
Appliance, Business Machines, Instruments	
Bearing, can opener	brass
Bearing, egg beater	brass
Bearing, ring; clothes dryer drum	new
Bearing, wringer roll; clothes washer	phenolic, nylon
Caster, swivel lock cam	brass
Coupling, motor; clothes washer	zinc

	Material Replaced
Pulley, carbon ribbon; typewriter	nylon, glass-filled
Pulley, return carriage; typewriter	nylon, glass-filled
Sliding surface, carrier in photocopier	nylon
Thrust plate bearing, watt hour meter	phenolic

Automotive

Bushing, pedal; accelerator, clutch, brake	brass, nylon
Bushing, axle spring	nylon
Bushing, steering knuckle	nylon
Bushing, steering column	brass
Bushing, valve sleeve; air and vacuum brakes	brass
Ball seat, steering	brass, steel
Adjusting bushings; power seat	bronze
Pulley, parking brake cable	steel
Bearing, speedometer dial	brass
Washer, anti-rattle; window	steel

Industrial Machinery

Conveyor fingers; commercial dishwasher	stainless steel
Conveyor links	stainless steel
Wear strips, link conveyors	steel, nylon
Roller conveyor, ring bearings	steel balls
Wheel conveyor, ring bearings	steel balls
Textile spinning saddle	brass
Window balance, closet door rollers	nylon

Hobby, Personal and Toy

Bearing, bicycle pedal	steel balls
Bearing, electric shaver	nylon
Bearing, and blade holder, pencil sharpener	steel
Bearing, slide projector	phenolic
Bearing integral with shutter, movie camera	new
Propeller, model racing plane	wood, bronze
Wheels, model planes and trains	styrene, iron
Bell crank, model train switch	steel

GEARS AND CAMS

Appliance, Business Machines

Drive, electric can opener	phenolic
Drive, hand and electric egg beaters	phenolic, nylon

	Material Replaced
Drive, floor scrubber	phenolic
Drive, tape recorder	phenolic
Drive, vacuum cleaner	new
Drive, voting machine	steel
Drive, clock and timer	brass
Gear, carriage pinion, typewriter	steel
Key trigger	steel
Sprocket and chain, instrument drive	brass
Wheel, counter; internally geared; adding computing, voting machines	brass, steel, cellu-losic

Automotive and Agricultural

Drive sprocket, corn planter	cast iron
Radio dial	brass, phenolic
Speedometer drive and counter gears	brass, nylon
Speed control, automobile	new
Rachet, brake slack; railroad	cast iron

Hobby, Sport, Toys

Fishing reel	brass
Focusing; camera	phenolic
Drive; movie camera shutter and film advance	steel, brass
Drive slide projector	nylon, brass
Drive gear and worm; model train	brass, iron

ELECTRICAL

Appliance, Business Machines

Bushing, terminal; radio, telephone	phenolic
Coil forms	phenolic, nylon
Gear; TV tuner, rotary switches	phenolic
Gear and pawl; telephone dialing	zinc, phenolic
Switch trigger; electric hand drill	steel
Handles; test probes	phenolic
Switch spring	coppered steel

Automotive

Coil form; fuel pump	steel, phenolic
Holders, fuse and lamp plug	nylon
Sockets, lamp	new
Switch, dimmer	phenolic

	Material Replaced
Industrial	
Arc suppressor; high voltage line break	new
Buttons, push; internally lit, oil-tight	phenolic, glass
Micro switch plunger	phenolic
Hobby	
Terminal supports; flash camera	phenolic

HARDWARE, FASTENERS, MISCELLANY

Appliance, Business Machines	
Cord clips; vacuum cleaner	spring steel
Fan blades; cooling fans	steel
Fan wheel; squirrel cage blower	steel
Handle, crank; adding machine	steel
Handle, credit card imprinter	new
Housing, lock; portable typewriter	brass
Knobs, control; electric steam iron	phenolic
Supports, shelf	steel
Twist-top control; sink garbage disposer	chromed brass
Automotive	
Cover, carburetor dash pot	steel
Fan wheel; squirrel cage blower	steel
Handle, door latch	zinc
Handle, window crank	zinc
Handle, packing brake	steel and cellulose ester
Housing, instrument dash cluster	zinc
Housing, turn signal cable	steel
Nuts, lock	vulcanized fiber
Nuts, traverse; power seat	steel
Industrial Machinery	
Nuts, anticorrosive, for aluminum furniture	steel, aluminum
Size checker, aperture board, for screws	nylon
Spring, postal scale	steel
Hobby, Personal, Toy	
Buckles, brassiere	aluminum, steel
Stays, stiffeners; brassiere	aluminum, steel

	Material Replaced
Slider; slide fastener	zinc
Combs	many plastics
Collet, electric hand tool	brass, steel
Fishing reel and pole ferrules, handles, collets, housings	brass, steel
Handle, portable radio	polypropylene
Housing, head; electric shaver	zinc
Housing, rifle sight	steel
Housing, marine spotlight	chromed steel
Key and mechanism, organ	wood
Lock, latch, knob; builder hardware	brass, steel

PIPING, PUMPS, VALVES, FITTINGS

Appliances, Business Machines

Container, textile treating agent	stainless steel
Dispenser, valve, actuator; bleach, detergent	polypropylene
Housing, pump; drinking water	bronze, steel
Impeller, pump; submersible, drinking, volute	bronze
Gear pump, replaceable liner; clothes washer	bronze
Valve, anesthesia unit	brass
Valve, drain; portable ice box	zinc
Valve, safety air mask	brass
Valve, swimming pool treatment	brass
Valve, water softener	brass
Valve sleeve; railroad air brakes	bronze

Automotive and Agricultural

Cap, carburetor; mower engine	zinc
Cap, fuel tank; chain saw	steel
Cap, radiator; automobile	steel
Connector, through hull; electric and water lines	rubber, bronze
Coupling, water hose	brass
Coupling, air; truck, trailer brakes	bronze, aluminum
Nozzles, spray; agricultural	brass, phenolic
Plugs, pipe; steering	brass, steel
Plugs, oil fill and drain; mower engines	steel, brass
Pump, agricultural spray	brass, propylene
Pump, bilge	bronze, rubber

	Material Replaced
Pump, lubricant; trucks	aluminum, brass
Pump, windshield washer	brass, zinc
Strainer housing, fuel; mower, auto	steel
Valve, cattle watering	brass
Valve, check; vacuum brake	zinc
Valve, needle; mower engine	brass
Valve seat; engine governor	brass

Industrial

Fitting, quick disconnect; drink dispenser	stainless steel
Valve selector, disconnect; drink dispenser	stainless steel
Ferrule, brush; bottle washer	brass
Tubes, bottle filling, beverage, detergent	stainless steel
Paddle, food mixing	stainless steel

Plumbing

Absorber, shock; water hammer	brass
Aerator, faucet	brass
Faucet, valve body	brass
Flush valve plunger	brass
Toilet ball valve body	brass
Showerhead; entire, or spreader plate	brass
Valve hand wheels	aluminum

INDEX